SEX, LOVE, AND THE PHYSICALLY HANDICAPPED

Also by Evelyn West Ayrault

Growing Up Handicapped
Helping the Handicapped Teenager Mature
You Can Raise Your Handicapped Child
Take One Step

Evelyn West Ayrault

SEX, LOVE,
AND THE
PHYSICALLY
HANDICAPPED

CONTINUUM · NEW YORK

1981
The Continuum Publishing Company
575 Lexington Avenue, New York, N.Y. 10022

Library of Congress Cataloging in Publication Data

Ayrault, Evelyn West, 1922–
    Sex, love, and physically handicapped.
    Bibliography: p.
    1. Physically handicapped—Sexual behavior.
2. Sex instruction for the physically handicapped.
3. Sex (Psychology) I. Title.
HQ30.5.A97   613.9′5′08808166   81-3085
ISBN 0-8264-0051-5   AACR2

In memory of Margaret Mead.
Her love for able and disabled mankind
lives forever.

CONTENTS

APPENDICES

Love demands all, and has a right to all.

Ludwig van Beethoven

PREFACE

E veryone is made up of physical, emotional, social, intellectual, and sexual components. Anyone without one or more of these parts is not considered a complete human being. The physically handicapped frequently fall into this category. They are pitied, looked down upon, scorned, and shunned. Society, their families, and professionals treat this estimated thirty-six million as second class citizens. By 1985 this group will increase by 20 percent. By the year 2000 there will be one physically handicapped person for every nonhandicapped person. This staggering growth in the number of disabled people makes it imperative that they be considered social and sexual, rather than sexless, human beings.

This book is an attempt to sexually liberate the physically handicapped by broadening the attitude and acceptance of them by the nonhandicapped. The term "sexuality" as used in this book refers to the vitality and attractiveness of an individual. The pronouns "he," "him," "his," etc. are used generically for simplicity throughout and are not intended to denote only one sex. It explains how sexuality touches on all phases of an individual's life, and determines how he relates to other people. Sexuality shapes one's personality, develops one's emotions, and determines how well one socializes. It is dependent upon a person's attitudes toward himself and his relationships with other people. How well he adjusts sexually is dependent upon how much he knows about himself and how sexually conscious he is of others.

School systems, rehabilitation clinics, and centers that offer sex education as part of their program for the handicapped are few and far between in this country. One reason for this neglect is that persons dealing with the handicapped are not informed enough about their own sexuality, and therefore are unable to teach and inform the handicapped of their sexual potential. The handicapped person has sexual fantasies, needs, and desires like anyone else. Frequently, this comes as a jolting surprise to their families and to professionals. The sight of a wheelchair, braces, or colostomy bag distorts the image of the person. It often is difficult for educators and physicians to realize that such persons are entitled to the same needs and desires as anyone else. Because there is little written on this subject, it is difficult to change the general attitude.

No one can be given a pill to develop healthy sexuality overnight. It is a growth process that begins at birth and continues through childhood, adolescence, and adulthood. This book follows this process and concludes by showing how the handicapped can and should enjoy healthy sexual relationships.

Parents, professionals, and the public do not understand that the handicapped are denied the most fundamental of human needs—the need to love and to physically express love. Instead, handicapped people are subjected to archaic and repressive attitudes about their sexuality. Only in recent years have professionals begun to examine the sexuality of the handicapped. For years, they confined themselves to the theory that its absence was due to a deficiency in personality development. Professionals who have made the attempt to free the handicapped's sexuality and enlighten society about it have been criticized. The literature that's been available is but a composite of scanty research, clinical in nature and serving a limited readership. It is hoped that this book is a practical source of knowledge. Such volumes as *The Hite Report, The Joy of Sex,* and the works of Masters and Johnson fill shelves in bookstores, thereby liberating the sexuality of the average, normal person. The same type of literature can liberate the sexuality of the handicapped person. This book aims to serve this purpose. If it does nothing other than impress on society the fact that the physically handicapped person is a sexual human being, it will have been worth the author's time and effort.

A book is the work of many people, other than just the author. Of all those who had a part in this book, I would like especially to thank Vicki Stetson and Margaret Wallace for their many hours of editing, and Penny Moorhead and Carol Newara for equally long hours of typing and retyping the manuscript. Without their efforts, this book could never have been written.

LOVE AS A FOUNDATION

All human beings have emotions, learned from the time of birth. When an infant enters the world he is introduced to such feelings as fear, hunger, anxiety, and happiness, and must cope with them to survive. One basic emotion is love, first given to him by a parent or nurse. As he grows into an individual he must consciously cultivate love.

"Love makes the world go round" is as true today as it was centuries ago and applies to both the young and old. Love is as important to the handicapped as it is to the nonhandicapped. It is necessary to every living creature. A pet dog loves and is loved; all human beings love and are loved in return. Any alternative path results in both human and world destruction. This potent emotion is the core of man's existence. It is food for the self. How one will live with oneself and others is dependent upon how strong the love instinct is. If one is to be on a give and take relationship with other people one must show love. Finally, if one is to express an interest in the opposite sex there must be the ability to love in one's makeup; otherwise, one is just boring, indifferent, unfeeling, and so has nothing to offer another person. This is true for both the handicapped and the nonhandicapped. The degree of disability should have no bearing on this, as the fundamental nature of human love remains unchanged.

What is Love?

On the deepest level love is an instinctive force present in the lifetime of every person, handicapped or not. Love feels warm when a child is cradled within the mother's arms. From this beginning a person grows to love family, friends, his country and, ultimately all things. We should not forget that love also means love of one's self. This is often ignored, yet it is so important for without healthy self-love, one cannot love anyone else. Love also means love of God, which is a love that sustains when all human relationships crumble.

Love encompasses the love between parents and children, lovers, husbands and wives, and friends. It is also expressed, for example, in a worker's devotion to a job, a teacher's interest in students and in a doctor's dedication to patients. All that heals, cultivates, protects, and inspires are expressions of love.

Some people die without it, for the will to live is impaired and damaged to such an extent that a person's resistance is lowered and he or she can die from loneliness. A lack of love can make people suicidally depressed and anxious. Their lives are like a barren treadmill, stripped of all purpose and joy. This can be true whether they are in the peak of physical health, confined in a wheelchair, or walking around on crutches. Physical hindrances in life have nothing to do with whether a person experiences love.

Necessity to Life

Whether a child is handicapped or not, he is born with the capacity to love and to be loved. The fact that he is disabled does not impair his ability to develop love. He learns to love just as he learns to handle the disability. All he needs is the opportunity. A child has to be nurtured to learn to love and to react to being loved. If he is not shown how then he will become unresponsive in life.

Good parents teach a child loving skills. They teach him how to give of himself and how to receive from others. His mother is usually his first teacher. A child will react accordingly to whether his mother loves or rejects him. From this first introduction the infant learns what love is and how to trust in a give and take situation. When a parent does not show love, a child knows what this means physically and later comes to know it psychologically.

A handicapped child who loves and is loved in return makes the most progress in self-development. Love can temper the impact adversity has had on him. If he learns at a young age to think of others, to give to them, he will be less likely to indulge in self-pity, or be angry at others because they find him "different." Most of all, he will love himself and have a healthy self-esteem. This is necessary if he is to develop to the fullest potential. Such a child will have fewer problems relating to other people.

A loving handicapped child has a better chance of being accepted for what he is by others. He is not objectionable to have around because his behavior will display a positive attitude despite the seeming severity of his physical condition. Regardless of age or his lack of physical involvement, he will radiate happiness. This ability grows with age and is vital to his development as an individual.

Fifteen-year-old Kate points out this potent need. Her family had little time for her. They did not praise or include her in family activities. They scoffed at her efforts of showing them her love and interest. When the author first saw her, Kate's facial expression was one of defeat and she did not function at either her fullest physical or mental potential. She showed little interest in her grooming and did not make any effort to improve her physical condition. "No one at home cares about me or what happens to me, so why should I care," she said.

It was learned in conversation with her parents that they wanted to find a living arrangement outside their home for Kate. Their requirements for this were high; however, their reasoning showed their attitude toward their daughter. "We are anxious that she live in nice surroundings; our friends would never accept anything less. Of course you realize she is a problem in our home. She seems to be overly sexy, and we cannot understand this. She is always getting dressed up everytime she thinks her sisters' dates are coming. Then she insists upon being introduced to them. This is embarrassing to the girls and to us."

Plans were made to find other living arrangements for Kate. When this was done and she was exposed to people who accepted her as a person and showed her affection, her whole world changed. Her feelings of personal worth improved. This resulted in her taking more pride in her appearance and developing acceptable social behavior. "I feel that I now live with people who love me and care about me," said Kate. The more she was exposed to such an environment, the more she accomplished. The sky soon became the limit as far as what Kate wanted to accomplish for herself and for others. Having learned to love herself, she now made the effort to love other people. She was less demanding because she felt that those around her really cared what happened to her.

The child who is not loved is a problem to himself, to others, and to his environment. He gives nothing and does not know how to receive from others. He radiates negativism and plays for pity from those who come in contact with him. He is a problem not because of his handicap but because of his attitude. Deep parental love is hard to develop toward him and often is replaced by the chore of training him. He is a disgruntled, weepy child. Although this may be tolerated in the home it will not be by those in his community or school. Even though he is still young, he will find nothing satisfying in life. While his family may put up with him, others in the larger society will turn away.

Studies show that human beings who never give or receive love will die. This is very true in the case of the handicapped person. The handicap has probably deprived him of a lot, but this doesn't mean he is worthless as a human being. His ace in the hole is to know how to love and how to receive love. Without this ability he will be ruined. He will be a total burden on those around him.

Result of Being Loved

The smallest child wants to feel that he belongs, that he is wanted and liked. This would happen from being loved. Parents' attitude toward the child tells him how he rates in their eyes. Sometimes, this is not true in the case of the handicapped child, particularly if his disability is visible and quite severe. Many parents have to work at loving such a child. They need to look beyond the disability to see the humanness in him. Since a mother's love for a child begins in the womb, they have to continue loving each other regardless of any disfigurement. This is not easy. It tests a person's ability to be a loving parent.

Parents want their children to love them. Therefore, they must keep in mind that to give is to gain. In the case of a handicapped child, the parents must seek out the person hidden behind his disability. When they do they are demonstrating the most important value in life that is even more significant than any professional advice. By giving love they not only nourish themselves but also the child. They will make him into a loving child.

It is easier to train and rehabilitate a loving child. His chances of growing into a loving adult are much greater. Limited as his physical and/or mental abilities may be, he can develop to his full potential. It is important for parents to be aware that an emotion can be expressed in an involuntary way. For example, an injured child can indicate how he feels by a slight voluntary or involuntary muscular movement. This is particularly true of the child who has a neurological disability. If he feels secure, loved, and wanted, his muscular movements have a better chance of being controlled. He will relax, play, and behave better. However, muscular control does not apply only to the child. How his parents touch him tells him a great deal. It can cause his body to relax or tense up. The mother transmits her feelings through her muscle tension. Her manner and attitude while caring for the child engenders in him a sense of either security or fear. The mother who loves the child does not have to worry, whereas the mother who rejects the child because of disappointment over his physical or mental state will have to resolve these feelings.

A child who feels love learns better in school. His I.Q. may be higher. Because he feels wanted, his learning processes are not impaired and he can be educated. While his disability may still be a problem to him, it is not foremost in his mind. He can think and learn without being hampered by the nagging question, "Am I okay in Mom and Dad's eyes?" Being assured of his parents' love lets him relax physically and mentally to concentrate on learning.

Developing unconditional love for the handicapped child is not always easy for parents. This is particularly true when the handicap appears at birth. Mothers are then challenged to separate their feelings of guilt from those of love. This is often difficult to do because emotions are often very intense. It is the mother who gives the child his first taste of love by the way she handles him; and by her tone of voice, she will teach the child to love in return. Essentially she is teaching him to exist in the world as a handicapped individual. It is the mother who will teach the three-or four-year-old disabled by an accident how to go on living. It is her love that will express to the child ways of coping with life. A mother's love, indeed parental love, has no limits. Its intensity is not governed or gauged by a drooling mouth or a weakened limb.

Five Basic Loves

While the love of things of the world, nature, and people are part of human nature, the love of self, parents, brothers and sisters, a Supreme Being and the love between a man and a woman, are the foundations of existence and all social interactions. For this reason we will briefly discuss each of these five basic loves.

Love of Self. Love of self is of utmost importance. Without it, a relationship with one's family, nature, and people cannot be formed. The way we love ourselves determines how we love others. It determines behavior whether an individual is alone, with his family, or mingling with others outside the home. When an individual's values are determined, his reactions to life then follow.

Love of self is one of the most difficult things for handicapped people to develop. They have a tendency to judge themselves by what they see in the mirror. If they see facial grimaces, an awkward walking gait, or poor physical coordination, they regard themselves with disgust. Self-love can also be stymied when a young person suddenly becomes handicapped. The self they once respected and loved is no longer whole. They sum up the effects of the accident on themselves. Without guidance, they will replace self-love with disgust.

Love of self is a learned reaction. Handicapped youngsters benefit if parents frequently tell them how nice they look, how well they're doing, or how they might achieve a skill. Praise does much to develop self-love. As the child feels satisfied from being praised, he will make an effort to help others feel the same about him. However, should he overhear those close to him comment on how sad it is that he is disabled, he will form a low opinion of himself and think he has nothing to offer others.

The youngster who has a healthy opinion of himself reacts in an opposite manner. He does not find it difficult to smile as people pass, to chat idly, or to offer help. He is not selfishly thinking only of himself. His troubles take second place to how he feels about other people. He doesn't need pity. He has confidence. His handicap is only as severe as others judge it. The way he loves himself determines the way his family or friends will love him. The barometer of his social existence is within himself, and does not reside with other people. The world does not owe such an individual a living; in fact, he owes the world as much as he can give it. Because he loves himself he can love the world and all creatures in it.

Love of Parent. This aspect is frequently difficult for the handicapped to grasp. Due to the needs he may have for parental assistance, he may not develop a healthy loving relationship with his parents. Often meeting the handicapped person's need for assistance is mistakenly interpreted as love. This is not true. Fulfilling the needs of a person is not the same as loving him.

The handicapped person should request assistance in a loving way. It is more pleasant to hear, "Do you mind helping me when you have time?" rather than, "Help me. Do this now!" The former shows concern, the latter demand. If he shows concern for others, he will also show them love. He must develop this delicate balance. The fact that he is handicapped is a primary reason why he should be loving toward those who assist him. When the concept of self is distorted, however, he will resort to dependency as a demonstration of love for parents, siblings, and friends.

Many handicapped people are not encouraged to love their parents. Too often parents let their emotions govern the way they want their youngster to regard them. They allow him to demand their constant attention. This prevents him from developing love and consideration for them. It encourages him to think that every time he opens his mouth his wish will be granted. If he is permitted to act this way in the home he will have a rude awakening when he goes out into the community. Parents will do the child a favor by teaching him patience. A mother saying, "I'm reading to your brother, I'll help you when I'm finished," rather than dropping everything, helps in developing his respect for others' needs. Knowing how other people feel and being taught to respond accordingly, he learns what it is to love another person. And if he is to love others in society he must first learn how to love in the home.

The handicapped person's pattern of love is often characterized by an overdependence on the mother and an overwhelming need to feel protected. Unfortunately, later in life the person may feel secure only when he sees everyone as a mother figure. This is neurotic love and is a problem in the personality development of many handicapped teenagers. The pronouns "I" and "me" are very strong in their vocabularies, and the pronouns "you" and "they" have little meaning.

Joan was a classic example. During counseling sessions, she strongly professed love for her mother. However, when her mother was taken ill and had to be hospitalized, all Joan could worry about was, "Who will care for me while my Mom is in the hospital?", "Who will help me eat at the table?"

Assuring her that there would be someone to help her while her mother was gone had no meaning for her. Joan wasn't concerned with the seriousness of her mother's condition. The "I" and "me" pronouns dominated her conversation. "She" and "her" (referring to her mother) were rarely used. "My mother cannot get sick because I need her!" was her main statement. She was unable to say, "I *love* my Mother and *I* hope she's not in pain."

Love of Siblings. This is one of the more difficult areas of love for the handicapped youngster to develop. He must, however, develop love for his siblings if he is to be a desirable member of the family. Without it feelings of jealousy, hate, and anguish may occur.

The child who watches from a wheelchair as his brother plays football yearns to join in the game. He thinks to himself, "I wish I could play too." He may resent not being able to do so. This is a normal reaction. Parents should acknowledge these feelings of conflict and help the child develop a healthy participatory attitude within his physical limitations. This can be easily accomplished by encouraging him to keep score for friends at a game, reading up on an activity even though he cannot do it, or making plans for a party to entertain friends. If this is not done, the child may develop feelings of inferiority.

When the handicapped youngster adjusts to his handicap, he will be interested in the happiness of other people. He will accept what he can and cannot do and still be enthusiastic about what others can do. Until this happens, the development of his love for his siblings will be stunted. He will be obsessed with the desire to outdo them. When he finds out that this is impossible he may develop feelings of hostility and hate towards them.

Encouraging the disabled youngster to be a vital part of the sibling's circle can be beneficial. The give and take among children in playtime can do much to engender mutual love. The handicapped who is urged to show concern for a sick brother or sister, or to show happiness at a sibling's birthday party, is well on the road to learning what it is to love that brother or sister. His thoughts become less self-centered and he is concerned about the well-being of his brother or sister. Helping him realize that he is not the most important one in the family and that he must show love to be accepted as a contributing member of the family is important. Accepting him as a normal child who happens to be handicapped develops in the child an inner sense of being a loving person.

Love of a Supreme Being. Teaching any child to love an unseen deity is difficult. Yet it can be a comfort to him as he matures. The fact that there is someone, whether visible or not, to whom he can talk is reassuring as he grows older. Loving the unseen deity can help cement in his mind what love means. To love the unseen makes it easier for the child to love those things he can see and touch.

Teaching the child the basic theory and principles of religion does much to give him the strength to carry on. This is often neglected in raising the handicapped child. Love of a deity supplies inner strength. It can help a child to live more contentedly with himself. If he realizes that the unseen diety loves him regardless of the way he may talk, walk, or physically behave, he will be more apt to grasp the true meaning of love. When he does this he will be more able to give warmly of himself to a brother or sister. Talking (praying) nightly to his maker helps a child to realize that there is "someone," other than parents, brothers, and sisters who cares for him, accepts him, and loves him. This inner tranquillity helps the child to feel more secure, less irritable, and more willing to give of himself to make others happy.

The handicapped person should be given some spiritual guidance at the earliest possible age. How he is taught to regard God is important. At the age of four or five he should learn that God helps him but does not do everything for him. He will learn what it is to love if, when he says, "Now I lay me down to sleep," he includes in his prayer, "Dear God *help* me walk," rather than, "Dear God *make* me walk." This develops the individual in many areas. It suggests to him that if he is to improve his walking he has to help bring it about. It teaches him to accept responsibility for what happens to him. He becomes conscious of himself. If he asks God to help him, he recognizes the fact that he is a person who needs help. This is a better approach than encouraging him to ask God to do everything. When the handicapped person does this he may have a tendency to sit back and wait, to do nothing for himself, and expect everything to be done for him.

If he senses that God helps him then he is more willing to love God for His assistance. This can be his initial training of having to give of himself if he expects to receive in return. Nor will he have reason to feel guilty. By asking God for help he will have a difficult time believing that God made him handicapped because of some sin. His concept of the Supreme Being will become healthier and the relationship will be comforting and will grow as he matures. He will willingly accept the fact that his condition is no one's fault.

The attitude the handicapped person, particularly the young child, develops toward God is important. His Redeemer can be a source of great comfort or great fear. Whichever He is depends upon the concept of God that is introduced to the handicapped person, and developed by him. A child would feel sad if he is under the impression that his handicap is how God makes him pay for his sins. He will feel he is being punished by an invisible person who knows all about him. He will think twice in the future before turning to that "person" for comfort and strength.

The same is true for the handicapped adult. If he has the idea that if God wants him to he would be able to walk, he might wait for God for this to happen. How much better it would be if he were thinking: with God's help I may walk. By this approach he does not place all the responsibility for his improvement on God. The handicapped person must realize that God helps those who help themselves.

James was a case in point. He was brought up to believe that whatever happened to him was God's doing. He was taught to believe that if God wanted something for his family all they had to do was wait and God would grant it. When James became handicapped this proved to be quite a problem. He told people that if God wanted him to walk, He would make him walk. James had no idea that he had to help bring this about. This made it difficult to rehabilitate him. He saw no reason to make an effort to exercise, stating that: if God wanted him to do it he would grant him the ability. This unrealistic expectation prevented James from making the progress he might have made otherwise. It was not until he reorganized his concept of the Supreme Being that he made any progress in self-improvement. He had to learn to keep his belief in God and still realize that he must help bring about whatever he wanted in life. He had to realize he has to initiate the effort.

The handicapped person should not use his misconception of God as an excuse to avoid facing life. Some handicapped people feel that no one will criticize them for placing so much trust in God's word. What they are doing is using religion as a cover-up for their own weakness. Religious rituals will do little for the handicapped person unless he is willing to pool his resources to help himself.

Love Between Man and Woman. To love a member of the opposite sex and be loved in return is termed a manner of success for most people. This should be no more of a problem for the handicapped than for the nonhandicapped. It is a matter of getting to know a partner as well as one knows oneself. Such intimacy involves mutually sharing hopes, anxieties, personal life, and developing common interests. It means expressing one's feelings with a complete lack of inhibition. Falling in love is exhilerating and intense. Infatuation, the first stage, is replaced by the wish for a new conquest of a love that will be deeper than the loves experienced previously.

Then sexual love between two people begins to develop. However, caution must be exercised for sexual love can be negatively stimulated by the fear of being alone, by the desire to conquer or be conquered, by vanity, by a wish to hurt or even destroy, as much as it can be positively stimulated by genuine love. However, it, too, can easily be mixed in with and stimulated by strong emotions other than feelings of love. Sexual desire, coupled with the idea of love, can easily mislead handicapped individuals into thinking they love each other when, in fact, they only want each other physically. It is important to understand that love inspires the wish for sexual union. When a physical relationship is lacking in greediness, in the wish to conquer or be conquered, it has room to grow into a warm sensitive relationship. If the desire for physical union does not stem from love it leads nowhere. Sexual attraction creates for the handicapped, as for anyone else, the illusion of togetherness, yet without love the couple are strangers to each other which can make them ashamed of, or even hate, each other. When the illusion of togetherness leaves they will feel their estrangement even more.

Sadly enough this is what happened in the case of twenty-year-old Terra. Due to the severity of her handicap, Terra had had little contact with the opposite sex in her early teenage years. This, however, did not stop her from developing into a voluptuous young lady; nor did it stunt Terra's sexual needs and urges. When she was able to attend social functions with friends her main objective was to attract a man. When she did so, a romance followed. Terra's needs to be liked, cared for, and to be independent of her dominating home environment, were so strong that she quickly gave in to an invitation to make love. She had not been coached on the do's and don'ts of petting and necking, thus it was easy for her to give herself to a man. She thought her bliss would last.

It was devastating and shocking to her when her "man" became tired of being with her. Her remorse was severe. Her opinion of herself suffered. She did not understand that since there were no feelings of love in the relationship, the supposed togetherness between them leads nowhere. And because the desired relationship was founded more on a sexual, rather than on a love, basis Terra felt estrangement even more.

The handicapped person who does not have a realistic concept of love will have difficulty relating to the opposite sex. A desire for sexual satisfaction, security, and the need to be liked, rather than loved, will be uppermost in his mind. His partner becomes a tool rather than an emotional source of strength and love. He cannot build the foundation for a relationship because he has little to offer of himself.

IMPORTANCE OF SEXUALITY

Sexual awareness is an important part of every individual's makeup. However, in the case of the handicapped person it is not recognized, and worse, it is ignored by parents, professionals, and the general public. It is easier for them to accept the handicapped person as one who needs care, rather than as one who possesses the same feelings and desires as the nonhandicapped person. It is often assumed that the handicapped person is indifferent to physical passions that are essential to developing interpersonal relationships.

The sexual revolution of the Eighties will reveal that the handicapped person is also a sexual being. This issue is at last being dealt with constructively. Professionals are recognizing that sexual needs are common to *all* people, including handicapped individuals. Therefore, it is only normal for the handicapped person to engage in sexual activity. This liberates him from a category that is centuries old: that of a person who engenders pity, needs constant care, and who is oblivious to physical feelings. To consider him asexual is devastating to his total development as a person.

A Destructive Myth: Second-Class Citizenry

Too often professionals place the handicapped in the category of a "second-class citizen," due frequently to an insensitivity regarding his basic physical and mental nature. This is also because people consider a blemish on the human body to be objectionable, and therefore find it difficult to attribute to the disabled person the same rights and pleasures that are easily attributed to the normal person. As a result, in the eyes of the public the handicapped individual is an incomplete person and is, therefore, characterized as second-rate. It is unjust to judge an individual by such criteria. Since the handicapped person does have sexual feelings, this places him on an equal level with everyone else. That his physical and mental endurance and capabilities may not measure up to the next person is no reason to put him in a second-class category. Everyone is a sexual human being regardless of physical and mental abilities; therefore, everyone is a first-class citizen.

Understanding the Public Attitude

It is easier for the handicapped person to reach his potential in all areas if he puts the public's attitude towards him in correct perspective. This is not easy for anyone to do. Facing facts is a good beginning. For the handicapped person to covet the idea that he is accepted, as is his non-handicapped peer, is unrealistic. Such an assumption can only lead to frustration, disappointment, and rejection. In general, people are not attracted to the imperfect. Again and again, the aim is to perfect anything within reach that is damaged. A crumpled car fender is quickly taken to be repaired; the minute a two-year-old runs his tricycle into the mahogany leg of the dining room table, the mother quickly calls in a refinishing man. In both these instances damage to a piece of furniture or an object is not acceptable. However, where damage to the human body is concerned one difference exists. Taking the body to be repaired is often impossible. Therefore, the handicapped person should not be asked to accept his handicap but be encouraged to adjust to it. However, this does not change the fact that the mother or father, or the injured person himself, would want to correct the body's blemish. To want to is human nature.

Even though the damage may be permanent, this does not mean that the person in that body is asexual. However, this fact is often difficult for the man-on-the-street to accept. Therefore, it becomes the duty of the handicapped person and his friends to educate others. Such education requires an intelligent, unemotional approach. Nothing is gained by trying to push unacceptable facts down another person's throat. The handicapped person can benefit by attempting to help others become aware of his humanness, which requires that he makes an effort to understand those who are better off than himself. He will then be in a position to help others understand the handicapped. If, however, he permits the attitude of the public to totally hurt, frustrate, or demoralize him, he will downgrade himself to a completely nonsexual, nonsocial existence.

He profits when he recognizes that the public pays attention to anything different or unique in men and women. All eyes turn to the woman who wears an exotic hat. Should a young lady walk down the street in a bikini, she attracts stares. The same attention is given to the handicapped. A wheelchair, a pair of crutches, speech that is unintelligible, or a clumsy walking gait, are certain to arouse curiosity. The handicapped person who does not let such curiosity upset him is ahead of the game. It is comparable to a smoldering ember: if you do not add fuel to it, it will eventually die. Curiosity directed toward the handicapped person will eventually die if it is ignored. Although an individual may find this situation hard to overcome he must nevertheless deal with it. For him to assume that the public readily accepts him just because he is another human being is unrealistic. The opposite is true. He must accept the fact that the public does stare curiously at unusual things. It is fruitless to try to change this fact of human nature. The handicapped person is in the minority, and must yield to the majority. If the handicapped person extends himself three quarters of the way in order to be accepted, the nonhandicapped person will extend himself the rest of the way.

How Others Think

The development of one's sexuality is closely related to one's attitudes towards the self, other people, and society. To be a valid member of society, the handicapped person must develop healthy sexual attitudes although this may be difficult to do. Ignoring the importance of doing this will limit his social and sexual contacts. The nonhandicapped person who conveys a hostile, overbearing, or aggressive attitude is not sexually attractive; furthermore, he jeopardizes his relations with people around him. Any anti-social behavior disrupts a person's social and sexual status. This applies whether a person is relating to members of his own sex or members of the opposite sex; it does not necessarily involve going to bed with another person. It refers directly to an individual being able to interact with another person, whether he or she is handicapped or not.

For the handicapped to force his personal plight on the nonhandicapped is unwise. People who encourage the handicapped to do this are not doing the right thing. A case in point is the recent upsurge of group homes in local communities. Some of these homes are accepted; others are not. If a group of handicapped people living together cannot conform to the behavior of their neighbors then the neighbors have a right to complain to the authorities. The fact is that when a tenant in a group home runs out in the backyard to vent his anger by screaming, it is no more acceptable than the wife who does the same thing during a quarrel with her husband. In both instances anti-social behavior is being exhibited and doesn't have to be tolerated by neighbors. If those in the group home can adapt to neighborhood standards no problem will arise. If the individuals are so handicapped that their behavior and appearance is objectionable to the neighbors then other arrangements should be made. Nothing is gained by pushing the problems of the handicapped onto the nonhandicapped society.

This is not to say that the handicapped should be isolated but it means that they should be given residential environments which specifically meet their needs and do not infringe on the freedom of nonhandicapped people. For it is when this encroachment on the freedom of nonhandicapped people occurs that the handicapped person's sexuality is questioned and criticized. Helping him to face realistically the attitudes and expectations of nonhandicapped people, rather than kidding him into believing that they are all blind to differences, is of utmost importance. Ideally, this concept of self should be introduced in the earliest stages of his social growth. People will not accept someone who insists on being pitied. The handicapped person must learn to conduct himself in a manner acceptable to the nonhandicapped person. For instance, a rickety wheelchair and dirty clothes are displeasing to most people. A wheelchair in good condition with a neatly groomed person in it is more acceptable. Body odor is equally offensive. People are receptive only to cleanliness. The handicapped person must take these facts into consideration. He should be aware of them constantly if he plans to enjoy normal social and sexual development.

How he is accepted by nonhandicapped people is up to him. If he assumes that it is difficult for them to accept him and starts from there, he will have better success. If the handicapped person realizes that he can make it easier for the nonhandicapped person to accept him, it will indicate that he is well adjusted. For him to assume the opposite—that just because he is a person, he will readily be wanted by others—is an unrealistic approach. No one is wanted by everyone. This is particularly true of the handicapped person. If the disability is minor he will be more easily accepted. If it is obvious to the naked eye and has an objectionable feature, people will be more apt to turn away. The latter he must recognize and accept. However, as stated, there is something he can do to cope with this. But it is the handicapped person himself who must do it, rather than assume the nonhandicapped person will do it for him. Should he find that someone does not want to associate with him he should not force himself onto that person, nor feel hostile toward him. He should recognize that some people may find it difficult to accept his handicap. Human nature does not like unpleasant situations. This does not mean that the handicapped as a person is unpleasant, but that his handicap is hard for people to endure. If he can minimize the effect of his handicap on other people then he will be ahead of the game. If this is not possible then he must accept the fact.

For the handicapped person to think he can go out and prosper in the world may be a fantasy. It will depend upon what kind of people he comes into contact with and how they accept him. It will depend on his ability to make himself acceptable to others. Sometimes this may not be a problem; other times it may be a serious problem. The handicapped person should take stock of his condition and determine what he can and cannot do, and make himself more palatable to the average man. He must recognize that some people will secretly wish they could go places without him because he holds them back. He should also realize that there will be people who, while professing to be his friends, may find it difficult to eat with him in a restaurant if he has trouble with a fork and spoon. Few people enjoy being with someone who spills food all over the table or who has difficulty chewing and swallowing food. A handicapped person is taking too much for granted when he assumes that because a friend proves helpful, he also enjoys being with him all the time. If he thinks of human nature he will realize that, in general, anyone who is well adjusted does not enjoy being in unpleasant surroundings. A handicapped person is being gracious when he warns his friends that he may have difficulty eating in a restaurant and that it could be embarrassing. If the nonhandicapped friend still insists that he goes then going along makes sense. The important thing here is that the friend does not feel obligated to include the handicapped person in all his activities.

It is understandable that normal people have difficulty accepting the handicapped person. This is not unusual and the handicapped person must accept this fact. He is being unrealistic when he assumes that every kind word and gesture extended to him is genuine. For people to extend such kindness is normal behavior. It is customary for the nonhandicapped to be kind to those less fortunate than themselves. However, this does not mean that they want to be around them all the time. Everyone needs freedom to go his or her own way and not be burdened, for example, by someone who needs physical assistance. This is particularly true of families with handicapped members. It is emotionally draining for a relative to feel constantly that the public is staring at his or her handicapped relative. Some assume that because they are staring at the handicapped person they are also staring at them. It is narrow-minded for the handicapped to think that he is the only one who is the victim of stares. This is not true. Anyone traveling with the handicapped person is frequently subject to public scrutiny. This will not change. Public stares can be minimized if the handicapped person makes himself as acceptable as possible to others. If the severity of his condition does not permit this then he must accept the fact and be content with a limited contact with people.

When he can convince other people of his sociability, his chance of being accepted by them is better. If people do not feel obligated to give in to him because he is disabled they will be more willing to associate with him. It is when they feel they might be caught up in his problems that they shy away from him. Most people will accept the handicapped person if they feel they will not be harassed by demands and negative attitudes. People stay away from those who cause them to feel uncomfortable. If the handicapped person can enter into their world and add something to it, then he has won a great battle. It is then that he will be welcomed and people will speak of how much they enjoy being with him. They will seek him out because he is fun to be with. For this to occur the handicapped person must come out of his shell and make the effort to please others. This requires that he forget his own problems for awhile. When he does, he gives himself the chance to appear as a social, sexual, and sensitive person. It is when he allows his handicap to dominate his personality that he appears as a nonsocial, asexual person. It is when the handicapped person gives the impression of being sad and melancholy that it becomes difficult for able-bodied people to think of him as a sexual human being. The fact that he may not be able to walk or otherwise handle himself physically plays a small part in this. What is important is his attitude towards himself and other people. If it is one of accepting life as it is, the handicapped person gives an impression of this acceptance to those around him. If he is withdrawn, hostile, and demanding, people will avoid him.

Interaction between the same or opposite sex only takes place when there is give and take between people. It is not dependent upon how one walks, talks, or upon how able one is in getting about or otherwise caring for himself. It is dependent upon how he can adapt his personality in order to associate with other people. This may be difficult for the person with a disability to do but it can be done.

Love for Fellow Man

Most people accept the handicapped because it is "the thing to do" if you love your fellow man. Or, last Sunday their preacher told them, "Accept those less fortunate than yourselves." This is usually a genuine reaction for most people. This is usually their philosophy of life. However, this is not always true in the case of the handicapped person. Loving his fellow man is often not part of his upbringing. Yet it is essential. For him to develop a humanitarian sense of love the handicapped person must love his fellow man enough not to allow his problems to affect the life of the nonhandicapped. He must have concern for how his handicap affects others. This requires that he give of himself to another person and helps lay the foundation for his emerging sexuality.

Sexuality is Integral to Personality

The role of sexuality in the development of personality has long been recognized. In its broadest meaning it does not solely concern the sexual act. It takes in all that is sensuous and beautiful, a person's self-confidence, his will to live, his power to go on fighting and to overcome any physical disabilities.

When the handicapped person has enough faith in his own lovableness and his ability to love, then he is well equipped to face life's adversities. If this faith is shaken by others' ignoring his sexuality, he believes that he is incapable of functioning sexually. The entire process of his rehabilitation is undermined. The door to the outside world must remain open at all times to the physically handicapped person. He must not feel that he is acceptable only when he has improved physically or has excelled in school. He *belongs* to the world outside too. This is the world he must become familiar with, not the limited world within his home or an institutional facility. This is why he should be encouraged to mingle with people by going out shopping or visiting restaurants even though he is on crutches or sitting in a wheelchair. This is the only way he can become accustomed to people staring at him. It is essential for the handicapped person to learn to function in everyday life and to acquire the necessary self-confidence which will prevent him from withdrawing into himself and hence immobilizing his will to improve and thwarting his efforts to integrate himself into society. Rehabilitating his sexuality is a natural part of this integration. The handicapped person should be encouraged to satisfy his needs for personal relationships, love and sex.

The attitude the handicapped person develops toward getting along with others depends a great deal on the attitudes of the people around him. Even the most severely handicapped individual needs to be regarded as an ordinary human being, to feel appreciated. A visit from a favorite friend or an attentive and kind doctor who has time for a personal remark or a compliment instead of talking down to the patient is of infinite value and can make all the difference in the world to him. It might even encourage him to read and study, to dare to venture out among people, and to take the first step into the world outside the walls of his home.

But so often, doctors, professionals, and family members, regard the handicapped person's sexuality as embarrassing or of little importance. Their understanding of human nature seems to come to a jolting stop when applied to the handicapped. The handicapped person only makes progress when he is encouraged to stop thinking of himself as a sexual failure and begins, instead, to devote himself to life-enriching sexual relationships with other humans.

The Beginning of Sexual Feelings

The nonhandicapped youngster, by virtue of his ability to get around easily, often comes across situations of sexual stimulation in his daily life. There's the school dance in early adolescence. When they get older they go to local discos. These occasions provide the first opportunities to embrace. They cuddle in each other's arms and dance to the latest love ballads.

For the handicapped young person this is often not the case. He must be satisfied by either sitting on the sideline as an observer or, more likely, sitting at home isolated from such social activities. This presents a hindrance to his developing sexuality. However, those around him can do much to help. Playing the latest hit songs on the stereo is one solution, or checking out from the local library the latest rock albums or tapes. Encouraging neighborhood girls and boys to visit and enjoy the music with him can enhance his social life. Encouraging him to attend community or church dances has the same benefits, and gives him an opportunity to watch physical contact between the sexes to help him realize that this is normal. This is why it is important that he attend social events. It lessens the chance of his developing into a nonsexual person.

Fathers can help too. Between the ages of nine and twelve, the nonhandicapped girl usually vies for the attention and acceptance of her father. She tries to catch Dad's eye in any way she can. The handicapped girl may not be able to do this as easily. If her father recognizes this it shouldn't be a problem. Putting her in the car and taking her to the nearest ice cream shop for a sundae gives father and daughter an opportunity to be together. Noticing the new outfit she's wearing and commenting on it is another way. Setting her out in the yard to talk to him while he works gives her the feeling that she is the only company he wants at that moment. Most girls thrive on this type of attention. The handicapped girl is no different.

A nonhandicapped teenage brother can also be helpful. If the sister needs assistance with walking or manipulating a wheelchair an offer of help makes her feel special to one of the opposite sex. By helping his sister he gets an early lesson in being tolerant of other people. Encouraging them to watch a rock concert on television together brings them closer. The same applies to the nonhandicapped sister. She can help her handicapped brother become sensitive to the opposite sex. This is an opportunity for him to exercise his male role. Handing him his sister's coat and his mother prompting him to give it to her is a gesture of a man helping a woman on with her coat. By this overture the disabled brother is exhibiting behavior suggesting masculine virility and sexuality. If he can stand up by himself, or is using crutches, he might be encouraged to offer to pull out his sister's or mother's chair at the dinner table. Again by doing this he is realizing the strength of his role as a male.

Misunderstanding the Sexuality of the Handicapped

We have all been conditioned by the world we live in to believe that sexual activity is the prerogative of the sexually attractive—the beautiful, the young, the able-bodied. Many in the helping profession who work with handicapped young people feel there is something ludicrous, if not downright disgusting, about their engaging in erotic play. When nonhandicapped people discover the sexuality of disabled people they often find it strange because they think such people should not have these feelings. They deal with this discovery by either stereotyping handicapped people or continuing to treat them as problems rather than ordinary people who happen to have physical, mechanical difficulties.

Sex can present problems to nonhandicapped people, too. For instance, the pregnant woman who tries to engage in sexual intercourse during the last weeks of pregnancy can relate to this. She and her husband find a way to overcome the problem. In fact, we need to realize that everyone is handicapped to some extent when it comes to sex. There are aspects in everyone that are unattractive to his or her sexual partner. Too often, sex is assumed to belong only to beautiful, young, whole people. Only when these attitudes are abolished will there be fairness for people who have cerebral palsy, spina bifida, multiple sclerosis, arthritis, and other abnormal syndromes. Then and only then can emphasis be placed upon, and something be done about, finding a remedy for the mechanical difficulties. Then people will stop being clinical and start being human.

Families are helped with their physical problems of caring for a disabled child, spouse, or parent, but rarely are they helped in coping with feelings of anger, guilt, pain, or anxiety. Nor are they given counseling on how to cope with the feelings of resentment, frustration, or ambivalence of siblings, or their own marital problems. The latter continues to be true even though it is common knowledge that the marriage breakdown for parents with a handicapped child is twice the national average. Of still greater significance, they get no help in coping with their handicapped child's emerging sexuality—with masturbation, menstruation, or wet dreams. This contributes to society's ambivalent attitude toward the sexuality of the handicapped. They quickly portray this by stating:

"They don't think about sex."
"They think about sex all the time."
"Give them the opportunity and they wouldn't manage."
"Give them the opportunity and there would be no stopping them."

"They don't need contraceptives; they can't get pregnant."

They make opinionated statements that are inaccurate but are too often interpreted as fact. Some professionals, particularly, are guilty of these charges. They work with the disabled because they feel more powerful, more beautiful, and more worthwhile working with the impotent and the unattractive. Some have the need to see themselves or be seen by others as caring or self-sacrificing. In a society that often seems preoccupied with sexual promise and unrealistic fantasies, very likely many professionals have their own sexual fears and anxieties. Unconsciously, they are aware that their own sexual performance and satisfaction fall below the standards that society presumably sets for them. Their anxieties are increased when they find that "cripples" may have sex more effectively than they do. This attitude is not unusual and should be understood and accepted if it is not to block the development of the handicapped person's sexuality.

Ideally, parents and professionals would like to think of themselves as not prejudiced. However, they may find this to be untrue in regard to their personal reaction to handicapped people. They may find it difficult to think of the handicapped as a sexual partner for anyone. For this reason, society is often afraid to allow the handicapped the opportunity to express sexual needs and anxieties. They are afraid that if he is allowed to express his sexuality, society will find themselves with an opened Pandora's box that they will not be able to control. As a result, they resort to the easy way out. They give dogmatic advice that perpetuates the disabled person's dependency and incapacity for making decisions. They force him to conform to the rules and desires of others. Because of their own biased attitudes and feelings, parents and professionals remain uncertain as to what they want the sexual role of the handicapped to be. Because of this confused outlook they have not been able to help themselves understand the issue, thus they cannot help the disabled understand it. Unconsciously, they feel that the handicapped person would be better off without sex or sex education, and that everyone, including the handicapped, would be happier and less troubled if the handicapped knew nothing about sex. They do not experience uncomfortable feelings when they can deny the physiological nature of the handicapped's sexuality; they prevent him from experiencing all realms of sexuality.

Sexual frustration is experienced by everyone. In recent years the overt use of sexually titillating material on television, in movies, books, magazines, newspapers, and advertisements has only aggravated such frustrations. However, the disabled person is often limited in what he can obtain for his own satisfaction. For instance, if he wants to use sexual aids or pornographic materials, he is dependent upon the willingness of able people to get the aids for him. Such people often make arbitrary decisions based on their own upbringing and needs. Therefore, the handicapped person must take into account the feelings of others around him and yet not feel forced to comply with their behavioral patterns. He needs the opportunity to look at the particular problems that dependency causes, to make decisions for himself, and to be responsible for those decisions. He may find it necessary to help the nonhandicapped person or professional come to terms with some of their own conflicts and anxieties. Unfortunately, until parents and professionals can examine their feelings and attitudes towards a disability, they will remain of little help to the handicapped person.

EARLY DEVELOPMENT

There is something unique about sex that has confused, fascinated, troubled, and delighted human
beings for centuries. No other aspect of life has given
more joy or caused more misery. No other natural, bodily, and emotional function has been subject to more di-
vergent means of regulation or profusion of expression; no
other voluntary biological activity is so personal and so
likely to be left up to each individual.

The handicap of a child can be so shocking and engross-
ing to parents that they fail to realize the importance of
giving the handicapped youngster basic sex education.
They do not recognize that this can hinder the child's total
development. It can result in his developing a poor concept of himself and of other human beings around him.
They become enigmas to him.

The handicapped child, like any other child, is a sexual
being. However, his sexuality must be developed in him,
along with other physical abilities which he is deprived of.
If he is to be aware of his environment he must first be
aware of himself as a human being. The unaware child is
apathetic, unresponsive to his environment, and totally
lacking in ability to relate to either sex.

Fourteen-year-old Carrie is a good example. Although
attractive and able to get about inspite of wearing braces,

she had little knowledge of her body. All she knew, for instance, was that she urinated and had bowel movements from a hole between her legs. She was terrified when she started menstruating. She was afraid she was going to die when she saw blood trickling down her leg. She had not been told about the normal processes that growing girls experience and knew nothing about human reproduction.

After ten counseling sessions Carrie began to have an awareness of her own person. At first, it was difficult for Carrie to recognize that she had the same female features as any other girl. The fact that another human being could be produced within her body was frightening. No one had taken the time to educate her to this fact. Her parents had treated her as merely a "thing" that had to be fed and clothed. Because of her birth injury her mother had found it difficult to cuddle Carrie when she was a newborn. Thus, Carrie had to learn at the age of fourteen the feelings of warmth from being cuddled, patted, hugged, and accepted as a sensitive, warm little girl. Only after her parents were counseled on how important this was to Carrie's development did she start to react as a human being. She became aware of herself and began to see herself in a new light.

The results were fantastic! Carrie began to do better in school, relate socially with classmates, and was welcomed into her family as a meaningful member. She learned to give affection and to receive it. Her teenage sexuality became a reality to herself and to those around her.

The handicapped person has to learn how to act and feel about sex. This learning does not occur in a vacuum for all his experiences become a part of the background against which the learning takes place. Just as every aspect of his human development is dependent upon previous and new experiences, the same can be said for sexual development.

To understand how the handicapped person evolves

into a sexual being, certain principles in human development must be recognized and understood. The fact that a person is disabled or disfigured makes no difference. His sexuality exists the minute he is born and is continually influenced by parents, other adults, peer groups, religion, the media, and other agents of influence. Thus he is born with inner and outer forces that impel him toward sexual expression. His handicap may repress this expression in the minds of those around him. Yet, and this is undeniable, like all human beings he *is* born with the right to express his sexuality.

Early Oral and Tactile Experiences

Keeping a baby fed and clean are not the only important concerns of a mother. There are more crucial needs of the baby that are met through direct physical and emotional interaction with the mother. The need to be touched and held, stroked and cuddled, is vital to the baby's survival and well-being. In spite of birth defects or other handicaps, the infant senses his mother's presence, her warmth, and her love most intensely. Most children learn this by suckling their mother's breast. The handicapped child may have to be helped to do this. If he cannot breastfeed because of poor tongue and mouth coordination, put the nipple in his mouth. If his arms and hands are rigid with spasticity, help them touch your bare breast. If he cannot put his fingers or toes in his mouth, like the nonhandicapped infant, help him do it. Keep in mind that the act of taking in, of incorporating, is important and characteristic of his whole relationship with the world.

Like any other infant the handicapped infant should discover himself as a social and sexual being. Sexual development does not occur separately from other aspects of human development. The crowning mental achievement of the young handicapped child is the gradual capacity to see himself as an independent sexual individual rather than only as a handicapped individual. Parents can help this to occur by encouraging him to feel his body including his genital area. If he cannot do this himself, help him. No matter how young or how handicapped, stimulation of a boy's penis results in an erection and a sense of pleasure. Baby girls become excited when they have the opportunity to become aware of and experience genital sensations. Such experiences of early sexual arousal and response occur in healthy children and are not different for the baby who may be handicapped at birth.

A study of children who have been handicapped from birth reveals a normally developed sexual identity by the time they are three or four years old. Other sources of body and sexual awareness such as touch, spontaneous sensations, and speech must be depended upon heavily to furnish the necessary clues for physical self-awareness. Feeling a toe, finger, penis, or clitoris and experiencing the sensation arising from it are important steps to understanding and accepting one's body. The handicapped youngster will respond as promptly to such sensations as the nonhandicapped child.

The impact of parents' attitudes toward the sexuality of their handicapped youngster is particularly powerful. Often, their first awareness that the child has sexual feelings is when they find him masturbating, which is the first act that prompts them to openly express their attitudes toward such manifestations of sexuality and sexual pleasure. Parents often do not understand that no harm, physically or developmentally, comes from infantile masturbation. It is a healthy, beneficial, and exploratory behavior pattern. When this is misunderstood, however, it becomes a sexual taboo. The mother may frown disapprovingly at the child, scold him, or slap his hand. Even at this early stage in development this can have a severe psychological impact on the infant. In families where masturbating behavior is understood, it is accepted and is not punished by the parents.

Giving the infant the opportunity to enjoy pleasurable sexual sensations is important to his development. This can be easily arranged in his playpen. If the child has difficulty moving his arms and legs, putting him naked in a playpen on a fuzzy rug with soft stuffed animals within his limited reach can do much to help him experience touch sensations. Hanging a fuzzy toy over him and letting it tickle his body is another way. These sensations and pleasures should be made available to the handicapped infant.

Parents should keep in mind that a child does not understand the reasons for their attitudes. He can only sense the emotions they express. Acceptance of his behavior poses no problem; disapproval of it has unfortunate consequences. The child quickly discovers that an act as natural as sucking his fingers results in angry disapproval. At such an early age he is too dependent upon his mother to endure disapproval without serious effects. Conflict then arises between the pleasure he desires and the pain of disapproval; he feels anger towards the frustrating mother, a decreasing sense of his self worth, and fear of his own sexual needs. The last two factors are a result of the child's helpless dependence upon his parents. He has no alternative but to give in to them and fear whatever seems to threaten their love for him. He considers his parents to be all-powerful and all-knowing. He is sure they are right and he is at fault.

Parents Can Be Adversaries

Some parents, unknowingly, hinder a child's sexual development. Toilet training discipline and the teaching of manners also suffer. Frequently, because the child is handicapped, these areas are given minimal attention. For most normal toddlers bowel and bladder control is a prime facet of socialization. However, demands for such control are often not made on the handicapped child. This can constitute developmental difficulty which manifests itself also in slow sexual development. Since toilet training has a direct relationship to the child's genital areas, a warm tone of voice and words of praise from the mother make such training easier. The child develops a good feeling about having his body perform according to her demand, which increases feelings of personal worth. Privacy during toileting is also helpful. When a child learns to be modest and to respect his body's functions, self-control develops which in turn is reflected in controlling his growing sexual feelings.

Discipline requires the same concentration. When a child is taught to behave and to control his impulses he will then also learn to control his sexual impulses. Dressing, or being dressed, in one's own bedroom, teaches the values of modesty, self-discipline and self-control. Impulsive, immature behavior, such as crying or uncontrolled giggling, is also brought under control and is later translated into disciplined sexual behavior. Conducting oneself in a socially acceptable manner is important. One is then also sexually accepted. Teaching a child to treat others with respect and dignity teaches him to also treat himself in the same manner. With no training in self-control a child will, handicapped or not, give in to sexual feelings when they arise, because he knows no alternate way. Bad manners can cause him to become socially unacceptable.

Becoming Aware of the Body

As a child becomes older he becomes more inquisitive about sex. Repressing this instinct can make him into a nonemotional, nonsexual being. Just because he is handicapped is no reason for him not to be curious about his sex organs and those of the opposite sex. In fact, this interest should be encouraged. Handicapped children are toilet-trained much later than the average child, which provides a good opportunity for the parent to educate the child. This can be done by explaining the names and functions of his anatomy. When doing this it is important that correct biological terms be used rather than childish slangs. This will result in the child having a better chance of growing up with normal sexual awareness. He will be more knowledgeable about himself rather than apathetically permitting people to toilet or bathe him as if he were an object.

Like any other child, the handicapped child should be encouraged to view his body with the same respect and dignity. He should not only regard it as needing rehabilitation. To do less would be to retard the development of his self-awareness. To encourage the handicapped child to think his body is as good as any other child's, a parent might comment to his quadraplegic daughter, "Your hands are so pretty and delicate, let's put polish on your nails." This will also draw positive attention to one of her good physical traits. She learns to feel good about herself, rather than just thinking she's physically disabled.

How other people go to the toilet arouses curiosity among many four-and five-year-olds. If a child is in a wheelchair, walks on crutches, or otherwise has trouble getting around, he may not be able to satisfy this curiosity. However, this should not stop him. Allowing the handicapped child to be present while a sibling goes to the bathroom can be a positive learning experience. He will realize that there are two sexes in the world. This knowledge makes him feel part of the human race. When he merely sits alone at home unaware of the various characteristics of the human body he is outside of the human race.

Adolescence

Adolescence is a poignant time for all teenagers, and this is particularly so for the handicapped. At this time crucial biological, emotional, and physical changes occur. The average boy or girl is able to adapt to these changes easier than the disabled teenager who finds it more frightening and often tension-producing. For him to cope with this stage of development requires understanding and support from those around him.

Many handicapped teenagers give the impression that they are mere children in adolescent bodies. Even though they may behave normally they are not thought of as "normal" by adults around them. Regardless of their behavior, their handicap classifies them as atypical, unfeeling individuals. However, if others can accept them as physically and sexually sensitive individuals, they will be treated as such.

Because handicapped teenagers are limited in their getting around with peers, adults often have to play a major role in shaping their self-concept. If adults pity them, they pity themselves. If the subject of sex is concealed from them, they think of themselves as nonsexual beings. When thought of as meaningful people, they will have a positive outlook.

Early Social Life

The influence of peers on the average teenager is very strong. Parental judgment is often pushed aside in favor of the word of a young friend. What is not taught at home about sex is picked up from friends. Rarely does this apply to the handicapped teenager. His learning is usually confined to his home environment. If the subject of sex is avoided by his family he will learn nothing. Their attitudes become his. He often has no way of gaining information about sex. If he watches male/female interaction on TV he does not relate it to himself. Why? No one has told him he, too, is a sexual human being.

The ways and means of sexually maturing must be made available to him. Contact with others of his age helps.

Prolonging his infantile behavior by taking undue care of him hinders his sexual development. He should be enlightened about the physiological aspects of sex. Showing him pictures of the various parts of the body broadens his knowledge. Naming the body parts as you dress him helps. If he does not understand what is said to him, assume that he does. Mentioning to him the attractiveness of his date encourages him to tell her how pretty she is. If he giggles assure him that it is all right to feel that way. Say to him, "She is a cute girl," or "He is a good-looking guy." This helps him look for the good points in his friends. If he shows an interest in a girl, he should be encouraged to phone her. Let him know he is attractive to the opposite sex despite his physical disability.

If brothers and sisters are talking about dates include him in the conversation and encourage him to participate. If you see the handicapped teenager showing an interest in the opposite sex let it alone. If you are shocked, don't show it. The handicapped teenager has a right to express his sexual feelings. If he is sixteen or seventeen and his older brother or sister has *Playboy*, *Playgirl*, or *Penthouse* in their possession, encourage them to share it with him. Most teenagers pick up this literature whether their parents approve or not. It is how they learn. The handicapped teenager may be so physically limited that he cannot easily pick up such literature himself. So if he can share it with a sibling or friend, do not discourage it. The important thing is to develop your teenager's social ability in line with the family customs. If the church is the main source of social contact, encourage this. If family socializing is more sophisticated, then encourage him to participate.

For instance, when he reaches eighteen or nineteen, nightclubs or bars may interest him. Many teenagers at this age attend them. If other members, siblings, or good friends attend, let him order a beer. At a church supper, seat him at your table and let him watch people socialize. Should a girl sit next to him and he puts his arm on the back of her chair consider this to be normal behavior. Teach him how to behave in any social situation. Tell him that it's alright to be a sexual human being.

A Supportive Setting

The handicapped person is responsible for the attitudes expressed towards him. If he feels comfortable in a social environment and at home, he will show this feeling to others. The public will accept him only if he accepts himself. If his parents and friends treat him as one of the boys, the public will do the same. If they see parents and friends constantly hovering over him because he is handicapped, they will do the same. If they see him included in the laughter and conversation around a table, they will consider him quite normal. But this takes time and is not learned out of a book by the handicapped person at eighteen or nineteen. He doesn't have to be considered "the poor little handicapped boy or girl." If he does not feel self-conscious about his handicap, he will not be made to feel self-conscious socially.

Seventeen-year-old Jim is a case in point. Needing assistance to function on a day-by-day basis he could not take care of himself and needed his mother to bathe him, toilet him, and otherwise care for him. She played a major role in developing his sexuality. Because he had the idea that, due to his handicap, he must be taken care of by her, he remained at an infantile level of development. Since emotional ties were not broken with the mother, he remained immature.

Being homebound did not give him an opportunity to associate with the opposite sex. His knowledge was limited to what he gained from looking at *Playboy* and *Penthouse*. Having never attended a public school or gym classes where most boys rap about sex, Jim knew little about it. When he tried to discuss it seriously with his brother, the brother was hesitant. "What are you interested in that for? You will never turn a girl on," the brother remarked. This caused Jim to doubt his manhood. He wanted a girlfriend. Like his brother, he wanted to explore and experience being with a girl. All he needed was the opportunity. He longingly wished that a girl would come within his limited reach. "I would love to put my arm around a girl and kiss her," he admitted. But he wondered how he, confined to a wheelchair, could ever do this. He resented being bathed by his mother. He wondered why it could not be done by his brother or father. "I have some pride," he burst out one time. "Other guys don't have their mothers bathing them at my age." He was anxious to be treated like a young man rather than like a little boy.

The best way to deal with Jim's problem was through family counseling. His mother, father, and brother attended these sessions. All three expressed doubts as to whether Jim could ever function sexually like a normal person. His physical limitations confused them. It was difficult for them to see that Jim had sexual feelings. No one had ever told the parents that he might have them. Their knowledge of his disability was only in the physical realm. Since he could not walk, go to the toilet, feed, or dress himself, it was difficult for them to understand how he could ever perform sexually.

During six counseling sessions they were helped to realize that Jim's handicap did not affect how he felt sexually. When it was explained that the sexuality of handicapped people usually develops normally, the family began to understand Jim. His normalcy became important to them. He was no longer an unfeeling, handicapped "boy" sitting in a wheelchair. Subsequently, the family was informed about how they could help Jim develop sexually.

It was later revealed that his brother was taking Jim to the neighborhood bar. Jim became quite a ladies' man. After the counseling sessions were terminated, it was learned that he had a steady girlfriend and had even double-dated with his brother. The father and brother told of how sociable Jim had become in spite of a wheelchair existence. He began to take pride in his grooming. He felt more like a man because his father or brother helped him with his personal care. They were surprised that he could show sexual love to the opposite sex. They no longer thought of him as someone with no sexual potential. Attitudes of relatives, friends and peers at social functions also were surprising to Jim's family. They soon realized that the way they treated Jim was the way others would treat him.

Being Responsible for One's Body

A healthy attitude toward one's sexuality is based upon how we accept ourselves. This is true for the handicapped individual as well. However, he often has more to accept about his body. If his arms or legs are stiff, or if his body lacks coordination, he may have trouble coming to terms with these facts. He may wonder how his body could ever be accepted by a member of the opposite sex. Therefore, he must be helped to look upon himself as someone worthwhile, regardless of his handicap. This will not be easy for him, but it can be done. By coming to terms with himself he will find it easier to accept himself. Otherwise he will live in an isolated environment with no contact with his peers. His sexual development will be jeopardised.

Parents should be aware that how they treat their handicapped teenager has a bearing on his emerging sexuality, which can be damaged if it is not handled properly. Encouraging the teenager to control himself emotionally is important. The fact that his mother may still have to assist with his personal care at the age of fifteen, sixteen, or seventeen is no reason for him to behave like a child.

Seventeen-year-old Bob is an example. His mother was totally responsible for meeting his needs. Though he could do many things for himself, she could not stand to see him struggle. As a result, she did everything for him. Thus he was not given the opportunity to get to know himself. His knowledge of his sexuality was nonexistent. His social, emotional, and sexual growth was closely related to his mother. He could not function without his mother because she had made him totally dependent upon her.

In the counseling sessions it was discovered that Bob had no knowledge of the anatomy of the opposite sex. He stated flatly, "No one ever told me that." He preferred to have his mother bathe him rather than his brother or father. "It makes me feel warm all over when she gives me a bath," he admitted. When asked simple questions about sex, he did not know the answers. His mother stated sadly, "I never felt the need to educate him properly about sex, because I never thought he would date." Because of this situation Bob was self-centered. His main interest was in his own pleasure and comfort. He was unable to relate to anyone other than his mother. This irritated his father because he feared his son was effeminate. Bob's masculinity was stifled by his mother. She overcompensated for his handicap with her constant maternal care.

Counseling sessions helped Bob to develop his self-awareness. He soon accepted the fact that if he did not care for himself he would remain at a little-boy level. He immediately wanted to do something to correct this. It was pointed out that *he* had to make the first move. Bob was urged to tell his mother that he wanted to do as much for himself as possible. At first this caused friction between them. Bob's dependence on his mother made her feel important. Once she understood the importance of her son caring for himself, they were able to work on Bob's maturing process. Letting him dress and undress himself in private gave him an opportunity to explore his body. A full-length mirror in his room encouraged him to look at himself. Although he could not stand up, he could do this easily by lying on his bed.

When Bob became familiar with his body, it was suggested he be given books with detailed pictures of the human body. This allowed him to familiarize himself with the body's functions. Once he understood his anatomy he then graduated to reading books describing the female body. He soon realized he was like any other young man. His sister also took on a new meaning for him. She was no longer just a sixteen-year-old girl. Now that he had studied the female body he realized she was sexually different from him. As he became aware that he was a sexual human being he began to have an improved concept of himself. He no longer wanted his mother to care for him. He developed a growing respect for both her and his sister. His father and he began to communicate on a man-to-man basis.

The teenager who is free of emotional ties with his parents, *particularly the mother,* has the opportunity to become a healthy sexual being. His attitude toward himself cannot change if his parents' attitudes toward him do not change. When parents mentally cease to be daily caretakers of the teenager, he has an opportunity to mature normally. The parents' lives will be happier, and they will enjoy being husband and wife first, and parents second. The teenager and all the family members will benefit when the parents express marital affection for each other.

4

PLANNING FOR ADULTHOOD

The word "adult" has a variety of meanings. It is often defined by the needs and wishes of the adult individual. A parent who does not wish to be deprived of his interests and activities may not hesitate to classify his thirteen- or fourteen-year-old as adult. Another parent, particularly of a handicapped youngster, because of his own wish to be needed by the child, may treat his teenager like a child.

The legal age of eighteen applies to every teenager whether handicapped or not. This is difficult, however, for many parents of the handicapped to accept. The teenager who is handicapped often gives the impression that he is physically incapable of taking care of himself. More often than not this is because his handicap is apparent to the naked eye, which can mislead people into thinking that he is also mentally incompetent. In many instances this is not be true. At eighteen the handicapped teenager may be as capable of handling his own affairs as his nonhandicapped peer. He has the same legal rights. The fact that he possibly cannot walk, speak clearly, or care for himself makes no difference.

Many handicapped individuals can live on their own with minimal dependence on other people. Like other people they are anxious to be independent and self-sufficient. Those who help him plan his future should try to determine how self-sufficient the handicapped individual will be as an adult. How much outside assistance will he need? Where can he get this help? How much does it cost? And where will the money come from?

After answering these questions, his needs should become evident. Can they be covered by insurance, or provided for by a social agency? The disabled person and his family cannot afford to ignore the fact that he will be confronted with such issues most of his life. Only the mature handicapped individual will recognize and deal with them realistically.

Foundation for Independence

Guidelines are helpful to the handicapped individual as he assesses his eligibility for adult living. Being realistic is the only answer to sexual and social adulthood. Following are some guidelines for this purpose, excerpted from "Self-Sufficiency Assessment: Planning for Adulthood," *The Exceptional Parent*, December 1978, pp. E10–E11, and reprinted by permission of the publisher.

A. *Physical Independence*—
   Can he live alone, with peers, or with a mate?
   Does he need the daily assistance, supervision, and/or support from people with specialized training?
   Does he need a great deal of help on a daily basis?

B. *Social Dependence*—
   Does he have any unusual health needs (beyond those that are similar to other disabled adults)?
   Does he occasionally need specialized attention that is related to his disability?
   Does he need frequent contact with health workers?
   Does he need ongoing treatment such as speech ther-

apy, psychotherapy, and/or monitoring of chronic conditions?

Does he need daily medical and/or nursing care?

C. *Self-Care Abilities—*
Can he take care of himself without help?
Does he require help with self-care skills from a friend or relative occasionally?
Does he need part-time or full-time attendance or nursing care help daily?

D. *Communication—*
Can he speak intelligently with others?
Can he communicate verbally with the system or via alternative means?
Can he communicate by means of special equipment such as a communication board or other electronic communication device?
Is he unable to communicate?

E. *Friendship Skills*
Does he make friends easily?
Can he make friends who are appropriate for his age level?
Does he need help on a regular basis in order to keep a friendship?
Is he unlikely to have interpersonal relationships other than on a transitory basis?

F. *Leisure-Time Activities—*
Does he have hobbies and outside interests?
Does he need guidance in using leisure time constructively?

G. *Education and Training—*
Can he participate in regular programs, college, or vocational training?

Can he take part in educational programs with the help of tutors, readers, note-takers, or special aids?

Can he participate in programs on a part-time basis with help, or without help?

Can he participate in specialized programs training handicapped people for the competitive job market?

Can he take part in training programs for disabled people for non-competitive employment (i.e. in a sheltered, workshop environment)?

H. *Employment*—

Is he employable on a full-time basis?

Can he be employed on a part-time basis?

Is he employable on a full-time basis at relatively menial tasks with low wages?

Could he be employed on a part-time basis in a sheltered setting?

Is employment unlikely?

I. *Housing*—

Could he live in an ordinary home or apartment without special adaptations?

Could he live in a home or apartment with special adaptations (ramps, redesigned kitchen and bathroom facilities)?

Could he live in a home or apartment with special assistance from another person?

Could he live in a specialized environment such as a community residence which provides some help?

Could he live in a specialized surrounding which provides substantial assistance daily?

In answering the above questions the handicapped individual will gain an idea of what he will encounter when he leaves home. If he understands what this involves he will have no reason to fear moving out into the world. Making such a decision will enhance his social, sexual, and emotional maturity.

Parental Fear and Opposition

Parents find it difficult to recognize that their handicapped teenager may want to live on his own someday. This frightens them; others don't believe it is possible. Years of caring for the individual frequently overshadows this possibility.

However, this does not mean that parents should force their son or daughter out of the home. Every young person needs encouragement and preparation to live on his own. This is a particular need of the handicapped. When parents express confidence that he can live on his own, and that if things get rough they will be there for him to turn to, they help stifle feelings of fear and uncertainty. With this assurance behind him the individual will make the effort. To urge him to do it just so he is like people his own age can backfire. Taking the sink-or-swim attitude can result in his accomplishing little on his own, which is what happened in the case of twenty-year-old Della.

Her parents were so anxious to be free of her that they told her bluntly to move out and make her own living. Although she could walk, could speak well, and care for herself, this was a traumatic experience for her. She developed physical and emotional tensions which affected her speech and walking. In spite of this, she made efforts to find employment, which was not easy. There were many months when she did not know where her food and rent money would come from next. When she asked her parents for money they told her that if they helped, she would never earn her living herself. They failed to understand that Della needed their help in order to establish herself independently. Only then would she be able to feel secure.

When efforts were made to help the parents understand Della's plight, they stated that they had raised her for twenty years and had considered their job done. They would not accept the idea that it was hard for Della to find a job. Since Della had above average intelligence and could get about by herself, they saw no reason why she could not do as well as her sister. Their twenty-year-old daughter was not going to live off them just because she was handicapped.

Della felt very insecure. The fear of starving, of not being able to pay rent, or of relying on her parents for help, was overwhelming. Like any other young woman her age she wanted to live on her own. However, since she could not get this across to her parents, she felt rejected by them.

It was obvious that Della needed a secure base from which to launch herself. This is what most young people need when they start out and what most parents provide. In this instance Della was fortunate. She ran into an older couple who were quick to realize her capabilities in her chosen profession. They put up money to finance Della's living expenses while she professionally established herself. Once she had a base and was sure she had enough money for food and clothing, she felt more confident about seeking employment. Soon she found a job and was able to pay back those who had helped her get started. However, she never forgot her original, crippling fear of not having enough money.

The connection between sexual development and the responsibility of holding a job is important. Being paid for his efforts has a direct relationship with the way an individual feels about himself. If the effort he puts into a job is worth his wages, he feels good about himself. If he is productive in his job he relates better with other people. The handicapped person who does not have the opportunity to hold a job finds it more difficult to regard himself as an attractive sexual human being, for emotional and sexual well-being is related to one's ability to perform in all areas of life. Like any other person, the sexuality of the disabled person is vitally linked with being vocationally competent.

The Public's Reception of the Handicapped

How the public reacts to different handicaps is determined by the severity or nature of the handicap. The person suffering from polio is apt to be accepted more easily than the person suffering from a neurological condition. Excessive drooling and flailing body limbs will turn a person away quicker than the individual who sits quietly in a wheelchair. The man-on-the-street will offer his help quicker to the individual walking on crutches than he might to an individual with a bizarre gait. He may be afraid of the latter. The person who wears a catheter, a colostomy bag, or has a heart defect will have little trouble. What the average person doesn't know won't hurt him; what he cannot see he will not react to adversely.

A handicap can be minimized by the individual's ability to handle it by himself. This means that if he is neat, well-groomed, and has a pleasant personality, he will be more easily accepted. The more severe his condition, the more attention he must pay to it. He should not think that because he is a disabled person he can afford to overlook his personality and grooming. The fact is just the opposite.

The following paragraphs contain blunt facts regarding attitudes handicapped people should develop. There are also facts related to how nonhandicapped people feel. Although it may not apply to every handicapped person, it does not hurt to be aware of such information. The following is not meant to degrade the handicapped person but it is an effort to help him develop proper attitudes so he can realistically fit into his peer group.

The handicapped person must fit into society. For him

to rebel and become hostile because he feels he is not understood gains him little. It is better if he can set realistic goals in life. He can only do this by acting emotionally controlled and dignified. A hostile attitude can cause his nonhandicapped peers to question whether he is a social, sexual individual. The ability to love and relate to people does not have hostile, militant roots. It stems from an individual's sound attitudes toward people and toward himself and his ability to transfer these attitudes constructively to others. He must learn to give and take with society if he is to join the mainstream.

Building Self-Confidence

It is sometimes difficult for the handicapped to be in control of his life. His decisions are often based on the actions and random choices of others. When his decisions are not based on his own rational choice, he is not in control. Being out of control is a menace to him and to those around him.

When his actions are his own choice he will experience more pleasure, less pain, and a better life. Being in control translates into having a clear mind instead of one that is cluttered, confused, and frustrated. It means enjoying love relationships instead of fearing them, experiencing warm friendships instead of being lonely, and it also means earning enough money to afford the necessities of life instead of being bitter and unable to support oneself.

The handicapped person who is in control usually understands life realistically. One of life's realities is that everything has a price tag. Love, friendship, a relaxed mind and body, personal freedom, and material gain, add pleasure to living. All these things cost. If a person kids himself and thinks otherwise, he is only leaving himself open to frustrations.

Most decisions that cost money involve other people, very often family members. Having to deal with other people is often the source of life's complications. Those who are closest to us can do the most damage. Friends, lovers, and parents are subject to human imperfections and, because they are personally involved with you, they may hurt you.

Intimidation—motivation through inflicting fear—is one of the techniques people use to get their way. If the handicapped person thinks about it he might discover that a large percentage of his actions are motivated by fear. It can be the fear of physical harm, of losing someone's love, or of being embarrassed. So he needs to avoid feeling intimidated as often as possible. One way is by asking the question: why am I doing this to myself? If he finds that the reason for his action is fear, he is being intimidated. He must decide what is right and wrong for himself, and then act accordingly. By the same token, if he can give of himself significantly to a relationship, it means he feels self-confident.

When he finds a person who makes him happy, he must realize that he or she doesn't owe him a thing, especially not love. How much love can he expect? The exact amount that he earns. In the same way, he can never enjoy the fullness of life unless he is willing to work for it. This also goes for money, friendship, self-respect, and love. The easiest way to ruin a relationship is to forget that the other person involved is a human being. The handicapped person must realize that people will hurt, disappoint, and let him down. If he does not expect them to do this ever he is expecting the impossible and is likely to get the probable—trouble and heartache.

Self-Esteem

The handicapped person who depends solely on outside sources for self-esteem, is less equipped to stay in psychological balance. It is more advantageous for him when he is his own star shining from within. In this case then his good feelings towards himself enables him to share such feelings with others. He holds his head high and thinks constructively about life. He handles with finesse the problems his handicap causes. He looks at himself and likes what he sees. He does not see weak limbs or a blemished body. He sees the person he is and he likes that person.

The seeds of self-esteem are sown in early childhood of the handicapped person. He, like any other child, thinks the world centers around him and, therefore, frustrations are inevitable as he starts dealing with the real world. If he lacks self-esteem, he will have difficulty forming relationships. He will feel inadequate and will question his abilities and the attitudes of others toward him. He will not believe anything positive that is said about him. His outlook will be negative and he will have low personal worth. Sometimes he may want to crawl in a hole and hide; other times he may become aggressive, engage in stealing, sexual exhibitionism, or boisterous speech to attract attention and to attempt to raise his self-esteem.

Responsibilities at Home Develop Sexuality

Doing everything for the handicapped individual in the home hinders his social and sexual development. How he regards himself is closely related to being able to do what other normal people are expected to do. This is particularly true when it comes to helping in the home. A sixteen-year-old handicapped girl, even though she may be confined to a wheelchair or a bed, can benefit from taking part in planning to redecorate the house, making out the weekly shopping list, or directing the weekly cleaning lady. The day may come when she may have to do this for herself. Being physically able oneself to do such tasks is not important. It is important, however, that the physically limited individual be able to direct someone to do such chores, which helps her to be mentally mature. If she can be around the kitchen she should be encouraged to cook, wash dishes, and if possible, run the sweeper in the house. Just because she is disabled is no reason for her to assume everything will be done for her. Taking part in making the home environment pleasant for her family can do a great deal toward making her feel a vital family member.

The same is true for a handicapped male. Pushing the wheelchair into the backyard and letting him supervise or make suggestions for doing yard work encourages him to accept his familial role in caring for a home. Allowing him to throw feed over a fence to feed chickens can also accomplish the same purpose. Permitting him to sit in the house day after day has no benefit for him and can in fact be destructive.

The handicapped person should be encouraged to develop the social graces practiced by the rest of his family. In some families this can include eating meals at a formally-set table, in other families a more casual atmosphere may be customary. The important thing is that the handicapped person be expected to follow the social customs of his family. This has a great bearing on his developing sexuality, for it is how we behave in these areas that determines how well socialized we are.

5

BORN NORMAL,
HANDICAPPED LATER

To have once known what it was like not to be handicapped, and then have one's physical ability impaired, comes as a devastating blow to an individual. His world falls apart. Once a total human being, he is now looked upon as only half a person. When this occurs in teenage or early adult years, the individual's life explodes into fragments. Putting it back together again is a difficult process.

Multiple sclerosis victims, war veterans, those with spinal cord injuries and those who survive disfiguring accidents, have to face the fact that they must create a new pattern for their lives. They need to take personal inventory to sort out what has and has not been damaged. Families must rethink their interactions with the individual. His condition should be studied and understood and his emotions kept intact. The health of his inner self must be preserved. That the injured person still has feelings and sexual drives must be understood. Relegating the individual to a second-class existence should not be tolerated. Accepting him as a person who just happened to contract a disease, or who is a victim of an accident, is important.

Psychological impact

The psychological impact is often more severe than the physical aspect. Studies reveal that the individual's psychological response to his handicap condition has a lot to do with how much progress he makes in rehabilitation. He needs the assurance from his family and friends that he is still the person he was before the event of his disablement. This encouragement helps his progress. He must realize that he is still an emotional, social, and sexual human being. Limiting his social activities, his contact with the opposite sex, or his employment opportunity can result in his giving up on life. The will to live and to overcome hardship dies.

This proved a difficult problem for Mary. She was sixteen when she was in an automobile accident and became handicapped for life. Up until this time she enjoyed an active, teenage social life and was popular in school. Her world came to a screeching halt when she could no longer walk, run, drive a car, and had to tediously learn to use her hands for feeding and other simple self-care skills. Like a turtle, she withdrew into a shell. Although with effort she could still dial the phone, she no longer called her friends. When classmates came to visit her she told her mother not to let them in and if they did get in she rudely told them to leave. Her current boyfriend invited her out even though he had to carry her to the car, but Mary stopped seeing him. "No boy will want me now. I can't dance; I cannot even put on makeup and style my hair anymore."

Mary felt the psychological and social impact deeply. When her physician suggested she see someone for counseling to try to rehabilitate her concept of self, she refused. For months Mary remained in a deep depression. When the author began seeing her she sat silently during her counseling sessions. When she realized she was not going to be pressed to discuss her feelings and that the author was willing to wait until she felt comfortable doing so, Mary was able to eventually develop the courage within herself to face and discuss her problems. After fifteen counseling sessions Mary began to think that maybe all was not lost in her life. With counseling support she gradually reconstructed her life. Her friends were made aware of her effort to do so and they cooperated. They warmly included her in their activities again. When she hesitated in joining them, one friend or another would encourage her and assure her she was wanted. This resulted in Mary eventually coming out of herself and making the effort to interact once again with her peers. Her sexual and psychological problems became less devastating to Mary. She became very adept at coping with them and not permitting them to affect her relationships with other people. Today Mary is married and active in her community and in her children's school.

Adjusting to Impairment

Adjusting to such facts as weakness of the limbs, loss of a body part, or a colostomy bag is not easy. While family and friends can help make the adjustment, the individual himself must bear the major part of it. Comparing past health and present condition is normal. However, this should not become a permanent outlook. Adjusting to the body's new adversities should take top priority. Achieving a normal lifestyle will be difficult unless this happens. It is imperative to control one's frustration and disappointment. Permitting these feelings to affect those around you adds problems. If the disabled person can take his body's condition in stride, those around him will follow suit. They will also adjust more readily and will replace feelings of pity with feelings of admiration.

Social Acceptance

It is essential for the affected individual to conquer his initial depressions. As soon as he is somewhat able to get around he should interact socially. His emotional and sexual health depends upon how successfully he does this. If he doesn't accept himself and socialize, he will live a lonely, withered life. His sexuality, previously developed, diminishes. For him to still function as a normal sexual human being, he has to establish a stable lifestyle.

Becoming knowledgeable about his acquired handicap and being able to discuss it is helpful. People take their cue from the disabled person as to how to treat him. If he is adjusted, and accepts the limitations his condition has imposed on him, his friends and family will feel more comfortable around him. His chances of being included in social activities will be assured.

Overcoming Negative Feelings

The newly handicapped individual must fight to keep a balanced outlook on life. He may find it easy to give up, which will probably be the easiest thing for him to do. Feelings of rejection, fear, and criticism, even though they may have no base, may surge through him. If he permits these feelings to gain momentum, they can eventually take control of every aspect of his personality. His once normal feelings of warmth toward others will slip by and his interest in others fade away. He will become a victim of an uncontrolled depression. People will turn away; others will dread having him in their midst. When this occurs, relationships become strained, to say the least. While he may continue to be loved by his family, he will quickly become an emotional burden to them. His social ability and sexuality will wane; the chances of his becoming a sexless, vegetating human being will increase.

The newly handicapped person should seek every means to keep himself on an even keel. This may not be easy to do. Acquainting himself with the organizations serving his particular disability is one solution. Getting to know others who are similarly disabled is another. It helps to be on guard against giving in to a defeatist attitude.

Upholding as many previous interests as possible can reap tremendous rewards. When people notice that the handicapped person is making the effort to continue as before, they will also make the effort to treat him as they always did. Hence, the individual's personality and sexual development will not suffer. He adopts a level-headed attitude toward himself, which makes it easier for others to relate to him.

A handicapped person's sexual liberation is dependent upon his self-esteem. If he is to be recognized as a social being he must want to associate with the nonhandicapped. This will not be easy, and it requires that he be at ease with himself and give of himself to others. Pushing himself onto others for their acceptance will gain nothing. Taking a back seat and thinking he has nothing to offer because he is handicapped is not a solution either. He must discover the happy medium and join the mainstream by trying to act as normally as possible.

The mature handicapped person must intermingle with people of both sexes. He must regard himself as their equal, and accept their nonhandicapped status as their way of life, and his handicapped status as his way of life. That their lifestyle does not have the same burdens as his should be of little importance. He will benefit most when he is satisfied with his own accomplishments and does not yearn for that which he may never attain. He should not impose the problems of his disability on the nonhandicapped. If he becomes militant and hostile, people will turn away quickly when they sense this self-directed anger. He should not make them feel uneasy in his presence. He should accept the fact that he may never do things as well as the nonhandicapped person. He will make it easier on himself if he can recognize what he can and cannot do. If he has to adapt, he should do so quietly and with dignity and not use his handicap as a showcase for his emotions. His main objective should be to help the nonhandicapped person feel at ease with him.

Is Sexuality Gone Forever?

Sexuality can only be affected, not eliminated, by a handicap or disease. Adaptations may have to be made in sexual behavior but not in one's essential sexual nature. Sexuality is an aspect of an individual's makeup that he can put permanent claim on. He is the sole controller of it.

Although physical faculties may be impaired, one's feelings towards others are not. Sexual satisfaction with the opposite sex is a personal matter that requires cooperation between two people. Mutual love for each other is the key. Weak limbs or a prosthesis do not cancel the feeling of love. Where there is a will there is a way. (The sequel to this book will discuss the techniques of making love.) The handicapped person does himself a grave injustice when he allows his physical disability to affect his sexuality. He is stripping himself of one of the most important normalcies he possesses.

Family and professionals planning the rehabilitation of the newly handicapped person should not forget the basic theories of human nature. To permit the handicapped person to think that he is less of a person is detrimental to his recovery. Assuring him that he is still a respected and sexual individual helps to stabilize his concept of self. Regarding him as an emotionally injured person, as well as a physically impaired person, is detrimental. Any person who lacks emotional and sexual vitality has no zest for life. A recent handicap need not damage an individual's ego. He should be encouraged to respond to his emotions and sexual feelings.

Living Normally

The handicapped person, by virtue of his birthright, must become a part of the mainstream of daily living. Within his limitations, he must try to behave like everyone else. His disability does not give him the right to misbehave. For example, if he needs an item from the drugstore, he should get it himself if possible. This may require special planning, which, nevertheless, encourages independence. Otherwise, the individual withdraws and other people govern his life. The development of healthy sexuality requires that the person lead as normal a life as possible.

Putting on a clean shirt before doing an errand reflects self-pride and dignity. That it is difficult to do things, or that assistance is needed, is irrelevent. The disabled person must first have the desire to do things, then ask for assistance. To sit around and do nothing classifies him as inactive and disinterested, and generates pity from others. Choosing to live in a sheltered situation over meeting the challenges of living in the world does nothing to enhance his social life. He can only improve when he is willing to interact with people around him—e.g., his immediate family, and the general public. This is easier to do when he is accompanied by a friend. As a result, he feels a part of the crowd, and gains in self-esteem. Negative factors brought on by the handicap are erased. He begins to see himself as a worthwhile contributor to the enjoyment of others. His "handicapped" thinking is minimized and he is respected.

6

SEXUALITY AND REHABILITATION

Professionals frequently have difficulty seeing the handicapped as a real person. Their treatment of such individuals too often concentrates exclusively on the body—exercising limbs and massaging tense muscles—and does not recognize the importance of developing the mind and personality. Moreover, professionals are also responsible for the development of the sexuality of the disabled person. During a physical examination this is seldom taken into consideration. The patient is put on a table, is undressed, and therapy is begun. Should the therapist leave the room momentarily the patient is often left on the table half-clothed. Frequently no effort is made to cover him up. This lack of respect for an individual's privacy and dignity does nothing to help the handicapped person develop worthwhile attitudes toward himself. Instead, it encourages him to think of himself as an object that nobody respects or protects, rather than as a person. This is unhealthy and damaging to his self-worth.

Fifteen-year-old Susan is an example. In her therapy sessions no effort was made to shield her half-clothed body. Because she was severely disabled and difficult to control, every effort was made by her therapist to handle her in the easiest and quickest way. Curtains to her treatment cubicle were not drawn when she was undressed, and if anybody came in to speak to her therapist during a treatment session, Susan was left exposed while they carried on a conversation. Such comments as, "She is so well-developed. Isn't it a shame she cannot make use of her body," were made in her presence. At other times a male aide would drop by and think nothing of patting her on the buttocks and saying, "How are you?"

Then Susan's parents noticed that she wanted the same sort of attention at home. This concerned them greatly. When they consulted the author, it was learned that the treatment of Susan in therapy was inhibiting the development of her modesty and dignity. She thought that exposure of her body was natural. The parents had noticed that Susan openly exhibited excessive sexual play at home, which indicated that she did not know what it meant to be modest.

When the therapist was consulted about this, she met the news with surprise. She was convinced that patients like Susan had no sexual feelings. She was disgusted when she was told they did. "Susan with those kind of feelings? She will never do anything sexually with anyone!" The therapist gave no credence to Susan's having sexual feelings.

However, when the therapist was informed about Susan's emerging sexuality, she began to accept her as a sexual human being. Soon she was able to help Susan in her development. The relationship between the two improved considerably. The therapist now saw Susan as more than just a body that she was treating. She developed respect and affection for Susan. "I really think my therapist likes me even though I have a handicap," Susan happily told the author. Today at eighteen, Susan is a healthy, happy young lady with an active social life. She is a modest, dignified person and a delight to everyone.

A lot of damage to personality development is done when professionals talk down to the handicapped person. He has the right to information about himself. This is essential if he is to operate at his fullest potential socially, sexually, and emotionally. It is his right as a person to function in his full intellectual and sexual capacity.

Negative Behavior of Rehabilitation Personnel

Sexual hangups among rehabilitation personnel often prevent them from being helpful to the handicapped. Because they often cannot deal with their own sexual problems their clients may suffer. Hiding behind the erroneous assumption that the handicapped are sexless is their easy way out. Frequently, they feel too threatened to admit that the physically disabled possess healthy sexual feelings. When this occurs it is debilitating to the handicapped person. It jeopardizes any progress the patient might make. It results in rehabilitative relationships lacking the warmth of human interaction.

The attitudes of rehabilitation staff can either help develop or damage feelings of self-worth. Not treating the handicapped person with respect distorts his self-image. Feelings of pity and disgust, unconscious as they may be, encourage him to think of himself as unimportant. His opinion of himself suffers. His desire to become as physically independent as possible is thwarted; his initiative to do anything for himself is compromised. Guilty feelings dominate his thinking. Sexual feelings that surface disgust him. To him such feelings are "bad". His mental, physical, social and emotional behavior is reduced to a level of inactivity. These attitudes can become particularly powerful and influential when the handicapped person's intelligence is average or above.

Handling the disabled therapeutically is a delicate process. If it is not done with care it can either overstimulate or repress the development of his sexuality. A cold mechanical approach, such as exercising the limbs, does little to help the patient. Such an impersonal approach can repress feelings for the self. The relationship between the patient and his therapist deteriorates. To the patient, the reasons for the exercise diminish; learning to walk or otherwise use the body, as well as possible, is no longer important.

A warm and friendly tone of voice between the therapist and the individual is important especially when they have such frequent physical contacts. The therapist should treat the patient as a social, sexual human being rather than as a nonfeeling entity. This cannot be stressed enough. The handicapped person learns to regard and appreciate himself by how others regard and appreciate him. The therapist may say, "How about bringing your arm up here," or "That leg of yours looks pretty strong, let's see how high you can kick it." This warm conversational tone is preferable to the mechanical motion of moving the leg or arm in a matter-of-fact manner. This caring approach helps the handicapped person feel worthwhile.

Sexuality of the Handicapped is Often a Shock

Members of a treatment staff are often taken aback by patients who show any personality or sexual potential. This is particularly true if the patient displays likeable traits. It is difficult for many professionals to accept the fact that handicapped persons are not always steeped in self-pity. Disability or disfigurement of the body does not necessarily mean that the person's emotions also suffer. Personality traits are innate in all people. This is just as true of the handicapped person. A patient who is pleasant and engaging should not come as a shock to members of a rehabilitation staff.

The sexuality of the disabled person should be accepted in the same manner. He is born with it and has the right to assert it. He can be sexually stimulated just as the non-

handicapped can. To view it as shocking is to play dangerous games with the emotional makeup of the individual.
To deny his sexuality is to deny his existence as a human
being.

Members of a rehabilitation team can either transfer
positive or negative attitudes to the disabled. They often
are instrumental in developing an individual's opinion of
himself. Their touch and tone of voice are potent expres-
sive tools. Healthy or unhealthy sexual feelings can be
transmitted to the disabled by the way he is handled or
spoken to. Since it is often the medical staff that he comes
into contact with most in the course of a week, they play
a significant role in developing attitudes about sexuality.
Should a professional's voice denote disgust to the handicapped person, he may assume that there is something
ugly about himself. If his sexual behavior is accepted as
normal by those rehabilitating him, his attitude toward
sexuality will be positive.

The same is true in the way the handicapped sees himself socially. For instance, if his therapist invites him to
have a cup of coffee or a cold drink during his therapy
session, he will feel socially accepted by him. If he is not
engaged in friendly conversation with the therapist, he
may see himself as socially unacceptable. Positive relationships with the clinic staff is an important factor in the
rehabilitation process.

The importance of those in the professions becoming
more knowledgeable of the handicapped as individuals,
and not only as case histories, cannot be stressed too
strongly. Occasionally medical specialists hesitate to recognize handicapped people as regular patients, due to lack
of knowledge or for discriminatory reasons. In any case,
there is a great need for better dissemination of knowledge concerning the various handicaps. A twenty-three-
year-old young woman is a case in point.

Betty, who had severe cerebral palsy, was in need of

psychiatric help. However, this was not easy to obtain for her in her community. Many of the specialists, when made aware of her physical condition, were quick to attribute all her problems to her physical disability and refused to see her. They placed no importance on the fact that she might have a psychiatric problem as well. The doctor who did finally see her made a quick examination, stated that her main problem was mental retardation, and gave the mother strong medication to control acute emotional problems. This solved nothing. Betty continued to become more emotionally disturbed. When finally one doctor did take an interest in her case and recognized that her emotional problems were hindering her making good physical progress, it was too late. The emotional problems were now so severe that Betty had to be admitted to a state hospital. Had a doctor been able, and willing, to treat her as he might anyone else coming to his office with the same psychiatric symptoms, Betty's prognosis for the future would have been much better.

· 7 ·

PICTURING YOURSELF

How we think of ourselves is reflected in the way we behave with other people. If we like ourselves the feedback is one of approval and satisfaction. However, if we do not like ourselves, it is one of disgust and disappointment. The person with a handicap frequently finds it difficult to like himself. The more apparent his disability is to others and himself, the more difficult it is for him to approve of himself. He has to learn to separate his physical appearance from his self-image even though they affect each other. Recognizing the separate strengths of both aspects is essential.

Parents, brothers and sisters can do much to help the handicapped person develop a good self-image. Words of approval and love from them will sow the seeds for self-approval. For a handicapped person to hear, "My, you look nice this morning," as he gets ready to go to work, can make his day. Such words give him something to build on, and puts him in a positive frame of mind. It minimizes feelings of self-doubt. His personality begins to take shape. He develops unique individual traits. He accepts that he is liked or disliked for what he is. He lets his emotions and sexual feelings come forth. His personality becomes controlled or uncontrolled. He relates to people and determines what he likes or dislikes about them. He begins to think how he might improve his personality. In essence he becomes a person.

How You Feel About Yourself

Feelings of personal worth are very important. Without them the person is devoid of many feelings. His sexuality lies dormant and untested. He finds it difficult to express warmth and concern for other people. He is mainly concerned with himself. The pronouns "me" and "I" become uppermost in his mind. He will demand his own comfort. These self-centered attitudes easily jeopardize his social relationships.

Learning that people will like him if he likes himself is advantageous to the handicapped person. He cannot afford otherwise. He must be helped to be sensitive to his own feelings, as well as those of others. If people are to like him, he must in turn show an interest in them. He must accept who he is physically and emotionally and not dream about who he isn't. His feelings of self-pity and self-concern will gradually subside if he comes out of himself and becomes interested in other people's lives.

How You Look to a Loved One

Love is powerful and can surmount anything, any handicap. Whether it is the love of a parent, friend, or someone of the opposite sex, it can minimize the impact of a handicap. However, the recipient of such love must assist in this miracle. He must recognize it, believe in it, accept and nurture it. Love can transform the most obvious handicaps. The ugliest body scars, the shakiest and weakest limbs become invisible to the loved one. What counts is the meaning behind the effort the person makes to express it. A touch of the hand, shaky though it may be, can express the same emotion as the most coordinated pat. The warmth of two bodies touching is the same whether they are handicapped or not.

Expressing emotion to another by one's tone of voice is often enough. Asking another to sit where you can easily see and talk to him serves the same purpose. A person who can express love without touching—by resorting to eye expressions or a tone of voice—is one who can love. It is not the body that expresses love, it is the person inside the body. Handicapped people will become happier if they keep this in mind. They will like themselves better, and hence be able to contribute something to others' lives.

Being Realistic is Important

The handicapped individual must display good attitudes if he is to contribute to society. How he involves himself with people and daily events will have a bearing on how he is accepted. If he acts infantile, he will be considered immature; if his behavior is mature, he will be treated accordingly. A mature individual is accepted as a social and sexual human being who can contribute to a relationship.

The handicapped person gains little unless he is able to accept how the public feels towards him. Generally, the reaction is one of pity, sometimes disgust, and often a desire to shy away from him. Many people are uncomfortable associating with the handicapped. The more severe the condition, the less he will be wanted. Many people find it unpleasant to be around someone who drools or has to exert to make himself understood. It can be wearing on people when they have to take time to help someone do minute activities or have to listen intensely to make sure they understand a person's unintelligible speech. It is more pleasant for them to associate with the nonhandicapped who do not require such concentrated attention.

People who will make the effort to accept the handicapped can nevertheless get tired of doing this. Their level of tolerance can be overworked. This is true in the case of parents, and is the reason why they look forward to the time when they can be free of the responsibility for a handicapped son or daughter. It is essential that the handicapped person understand that the average individual does not altogether know what it is like to be handicapped. The handicapped person must realize that his disability may be heartbreaking to his parents, spouse, relatives and friends. Nobody wants a handicapped person in his or her family. The disabled person will grow in admitting that it is unfortunate for his family to have to cope with him and his handicap. When he can do this without self-pity, his family will find it easier to accept him. They will realize that he understands their feelings and the problems they have in coping with him, a handicapped person. The handicapped must accept as fact that some people can endure the handicapped more than others, and that they stand to fear that a handicapped person is socially detrimental to them.

This was true in the case of Carol. She was the older of two girls, and was well-educated and successful in the arts. But this was not impressive enough for her younger sister, Sally, who was very conscious of the fact that she had a handicapped sister. When it came to including Carol in social events, she was hesitant. Even though her friends were the first to tell her how much they enjoyed Carol's company, this was not enough assurance. The fact that Carol needed assistance in walking was a big problem to Sally. She was worried about what other people thought about her.

At first it was difficult for Carol to adjust to her sister's attitude. As she grew older she understood how and why Sally felt as she did. Carol had to rise above her own feelings and make the best of the way Sally treated her. She realized that she only added to Sally's unhappiness by asking her assistance, and had to accept the fact that Sally brought her children up to think of their aunt as a burden.

Carol had to face the fact that Sally had transferred her own attitudes to her children. She had to accept that no matter how successful she was in her career, her sister would never accept her. In counseling sessions Carol was able to adjust to the fact that Sally would only be able to accept her if she could become unhandicapped. This, of course, was impossible. Carol was deeply hurt. She had to accept the painful fact that Sally would never be happy with her. Further counseling sessions revealed that Sally had been raised to think this way by their parents. Carol's case illustrates the importance of families realizing that the way they treat a handicapped person is the way nonhandicapped siblings learn to treat them later in life.

Another related point concerns recognizing the difference between someone's genuine effort to build a friendship and his friendly gestures because he "feels sorry" for the handicapped person. It is important for the handicapped to not leap at every person who wants to be his friend. It is wise to consider why someone wants to befriend him. The mature and well-adjusted handicapped person is mindful of this. He should not alienate himself from people either. People who talk to, and not down to, him are trustworthy. They, rather than being overbearing with their help, by instinct resist lending a hand to the handicapped person unless asked. Their quality of conversation is a factor also. The handicapped feels at ease when he knows the person does not feel pity for him but wants to get to know him for what he has to offer to a friendship.

If the handicapped person is discriminating in his choice of companions, he will be more likely to develop concrete friendships. The average person can quickly tell whether the handicapped person is a normal, social individual. When the disabled person can discreetly convey the effect his handicap may have on the average person, he is more readily accepted. He only fools himself in pretending that everyone he comes into contact with accepts him. It is understandable that many people cannot help feeling pity for him and will therefore want to get away quickly into "normal" surroundings. The handicapped person may be able to win over some of these people; others will not succumb so easily. It will depend upon people's common likes and dislikes. Some find it easier to accept adversities in life than others. The handicapped person is no different. Some are more broad-minded than others about their condition. Life is difficult for the handicapped person who chooses to be self-centered and looks for others to care for him and to grant his every demand. Such a person will never feel fully wanted by other people. People around him will continually be sceptical about his intelligence, his social ability including sexuality. This makes it even more difficult for him to find his niche in life.

Since the handicapped person is in the minority he is forced to act accordingly and yield to the majority. The nonhandicapped world does not owe him a living. Like everyone else, he owes society as much as he can give, within his particular limitations. He is at fault when he continually looks to see what others can give him for he will only get from life what he puts into it.

The handicapped person cannot go wrong if he is realistic about himself and his place in society. If he readily admits he cannot do a task and does not struggle to prove otherwise, he is being honest and realistic. If he discovers that he cannot do his job and tells his employer immediately, it shows he is well-adjusted to his disability. The person who takes a job that is too difficult for him to do, and as a result lowers the company's productivity, is thoughtless and also unrealistic. He should not look to an employer to make adjustments just so he can have a job. If he fills a job's requirements, all well and good; if he doesn't, then he should admit it and seek employment elsewhere.

Consider the disabled person who says, "Oh, no. You go ahead. I walk too slow. If you wait for me, you will never get your shopping done." This person is realistic. His companionship will be sought out more readily. He does not impose his limitations on others for personal benefit. The same is true of the handicapped woman who advises her nonhandicapped fiance, before they marry, to consider the effect her condition may have on his future. She is sensitive to her spouse's welfare and places her own hopes and dreams second to his life and future. This strengthens the relationship and helps it to work out. The communication ties between the two are reinforced.

A handicapped person who decides not to drive a car because of poorly coordinated limbs is realistic about his capabilities. It should be understood that a handicapped person cannot always fulfill his most profound wish or dream. His handicap will determine what is advisable to do. He can and should transfer the same ability to adapt to other areas of his life.

Presenting Yourself in the World

We all seek society's acceptance. The handicapped person does, too. However, he has to learn the skills to gain such acceptance. To obtain this he cannot afford to be aloof, nor overly aggressive. People are turned off when someone is shy or aggressive. Usually, they look at a face first before the body. When the facial expression is pleasant, people assume that he is a well-adjusted individual. They have no difficulty accepting him as a total human being, regardless of whether he is on crutches, in a wheelchair, or bedridden.

The handicapped person should not hesitate to behave like everyone else. For instance, the handicapped girl who engages a nonhandicapped man in conversation is expressing the same sexual awareness as would any other girl. This very act is an indication that she recognizes the concept of the two sexes. When this is observed by those around her, they think of her as normal.

How people present themselves to the world makes an indelible impression. The impression the handicapped present can be either warm or without feeling. Conversation also tells a lot about a person: how he feels and how and what he thinks. If it is self-centered the public will shy away. If it is, for example, about a news item, rather than about himself, people are more apt to listen. Concentrating on making others feel good about themselves is a good idea. Making crude remarks to assure membership in a group never works. The handicapped person who insists upon doing this risks being scoffed at. Often it is interpreted as a tasteless overture to get sexual attention. He will make a better impression when he conducts himself as an emotionally mature adult. His appeal is more apt to come across and be noticed by others if he is careful in his approach. This is not to cancel out sexual banter between friends. It is to emphasize that it is important that the handicapped individual conduct himself in a dignified manner at public events. Anything less brands him and his handicapped peers negatively.

Telling dirty jokes or making off-the-cuff sexual remarks does not show one's sexuality in a good light. This is true for everyone. Perhaps it is important to refrain from such comments altogether. To be recognized as a sexual human being, it is more effective to follow the norms of social behavior. The woman who dresses conspicuously to attract attention gains little. While she may be whistled at or commented upon, her chances of being truly accepted are slim. Excessive erotic play in public between the sexes meets with the same opposition. The handicapped couple should be discreet. Otherwise, they leave themselves open to criticism, maybe more so than their non-handicapped peers.

8

JOINING THE CROWD

The daily life of most young people involves being around others, at home, in school, and on the street. This is not always true for the handicapped person. He may find it difficult to get out of the house because of his handicap. As a result his contact with the public is limited. He lacks the opportunity to rub shoulders with his peers, to listen to them talk about things, about sex. He is restricted from normal sexual contact. This does not refer to sexual stimulation from body-to-body contact, but to socializing with others, particularly of the opposite sex.

The person with a handicap may feel shy about being with people. He may feel unwanted because he is unable to get around, talk, or physically behave like other people. Sometimes this is true, not always. The handicapped person should realize that he has control over whether he is or is not accepted. He does not have to talk or walk normally to be liked. A person with a clumsy gait or who sits in a wheelchair can be as sociable as a normal person. The important thing is to want to associate with people. When he can do this, he will be more able to develop into a sexually normal person.

Expressing Warmth and Feelings

If a handicapped person continues to feel self-conscious about his condition, he will have difficulty entering the mainstream of life. By first accepting his condition, then concentrating on becoming a part of the crowd he will benefit. Showing interest in other people's lives is a sure way. This can result in a handicapped person's tense muscles relaxing, and his feelings of inadequacy will become minimized. He will feel good about himself and find it easier to exert himself to make others happy and show concern for their welfare. Hence, he will be considered a normal individual, with sexual feelings. Failure to do this blocks his social integration.

Forming Social Ties

As with any person, the development of the handicapped person's sexuality requires associating with others. If the individual is employed this usually takes care of itself. On-the-job relationships with co-workers stimulate social and sexual growth. When the handicapped person fears forming social ties, his growth and success on the job is affected.

The warmth that results from relationships formed at church often cannot be matched. Such an environment can help cement lasting social relationships for the handicapped. However, these do not just happen. Offering to help on church committees, sharing a Sunday school class, or making other contributions has its rewards. Merely going to church every Sunday morning is not the way. Within the circle of the church family, the handicapped can find much warmth in social contacts. He is unlikely to be turned away. He can practice being sociable, feel compassion for others, and has the opportunity to act as a full, sexual human being. He will meet people, be mentally stimulated, and become acclimated to social interaction. Nowadays, churches are making attendance more possible for the handicapped by installing ramps for wheelchairs and street-level entrances. All he has to do is to take advantage of these opportunities.

Community resources should not be off-limits to the handicapped. If it is possible for him to go shopping, he should do so. Nothing is gained by having other people buy clothes or other items for him. He can learn much from being a part of the hustle and bustle of a supermarket or a department store. Submitting himself to it can help him overcome feelings of self-consciousness and/or inferiority. However, the handicapped individual must do it for *himself* and *not* the public. No one can do it for him. Confinement to the home does not pay off. He must learn to face life in the street. For the handicapped person to hear another person say, "Excuse me," if he bumps into him is rewarding. He becomes aware that people find him important enough to say, "Excuse me." This is important to the handicapped person's sense of worth, which does not occur when he is cut off from society. It is these experiences that help create for him his self-awareness as a social, and sexual, individual.

Beth is a good example of what can happen when the handicapped person comes out of his or her shell. At the age of sixteen she was becoming a recluse. She had everything a girl could want. Nevertheless, she lacked interaction with society. Her family did not help in this respect, because they were afraid she would get hurt—physically, mentally, and emotionally. Yet Beth's depression and melancholy were of concern to them, so they consulted the author for counseling.

Beth wanted to get out and be with other people. She resented being confined to the company of her mother, father, and two sisters. She yearned to know how the rest of the world lived. She was not afraid to meet others but was sensitive to her family's fears about her doing so. "Because I am handicapped must I always live at home and not be with other people?" she wondered. She resented being left home in the evening to watch TV while her sisters went out with friends and her parents next door to play pinochle. During such times feelings of depression overwhelmed Beth. Though she could not walk she considered herself no different from other people. Encouraging the family to let Beth attend church functions and go shopping for her own clothes helped a lot. Her parents were counseled against sheltering her from exposure to the normal world. The importance of letting her experience the pros and cons of being a handicapped person was emphasized. Beth became more at ease with others. Once the initial breakthrough into social interaction was made, she began to cope with the problems that her handicap imposed. Soon she was receiving phone calls and friends were dropping in to see her.

As she blossomed under this new experience one young man asked her for a date. Because she was relaxed, her pleasant wit and personality bloomed. It was no problem to him to have to push her in a wheelchair and lift her in and out of his car. He enjoyed being with her and did not find her handicap to be an obstacle. This relationship gave her the experience of socializing on a one-to-one basis with the opposite sex.

Marriage was not Beth's wish at this time. She was merely experiencing the social interchange that is common to all adolescents. This could have remained dormant for years had she and her family not sought counseling. Her mother was pleased to instruct Beth on the do's and don'ts of dating. She never thought she would have these worries concerning her handicapped daughter. "Beth has the same sexual feelings as my other teenage daughters," the mother realized. In the eyes of her family Beth took on a new dimension. She was only physically dependent on them, not emotionally or mentally.

The sexuality of the handicapped can either remain dormant or it regresses to dormancy. The reasons for this vary. Attitudes toward the handicapped is one. Judging him as asexual is another. This can result in the failure to encourage him to interact with his peers and with society. This can strip him of all reason for exerting social, emotional, and sexual feelings. Rubbing shoulders with other people, coping with flirtatious glances in a store, and weaving through a crowd at rush hour helps to stimulate a person's sexuality. Men and women learn to cope with each other. The handicapped person should not feel that a physical handicap deprives him of this experience; his sexuality continues to develop regardless of it. The only detriment to the disabled individual is when he does not take advantage of coming into contact with others.

Communicating Physically

In the area of communicating physically the handicapped person may have to make adaptations in his sexual behavior. If he is confined to a wheelchair, wears braces, has a catheter, or walks on crutches, his sexual activity may have to be planned in a realistic way. If both partners are in wheelchairs, they will have to plan the position in which they can touch, hug, or kiss each other. They have to take into consideration how much each is able to move in their chairs. Can they lean forward? Can they stretch their arms out to touch each other? Could one or the other hold his or her partner on his lap? When these hindrances are solved, then they can proceed further. Sitting facing each other with their wheelchairs parallel makes eye contact and holding hands easier. Whatever the position chosen, each partner should enjoy fully the moments of togetherness. When the handicapped person permits a lack of planning to interfere with normal sexual expression, he deprives himself and his partner of a warm, satisfying relationship.

If the disabled person wears braces, then some other plan is necessary. If the person has cerebral palsy, he may have tense arms and legs. In this case the partners have to talk about what they want to accomplish, then tell each other of his or her problems that could hinder expressions of affection. If one partner reaches tenderly for a hand, but due to involuntary muscle spasms grabs it roughly, this may startle his or her partner. However, if the partner explains this to the loved one, it will probably be accepted warmly. If one partner is in a full body brace, the other may have to do most of the physical activity. The important thing is that nothing interferes with their expressing sexuality.

Dating

The handicapped individual should not be restricted to just dating another handicapped person. If he happens to function socially and can relate sexually to the nonhandicapped, he should do so. He should not be discouraged if he does attract a nonhandicapped person. It is possible that a handicapped person can be attractive to the nonhandicapped. However, this should not be considered all-important. The handicapped person who feels more comfortable with another handicapped partner can be just as happy. Who a person dates should be left to individual choice. People do not choose each other because they both have brown hair or other characteristics that are alike. While it is important that dating partners be compatible, the compatibility should not be determined by physical ability. It should stem from how each partner responds to the other on an emotional, social and sexual level. A nonhandicapped man may find endearing qualities in the co-worker in his office. The fact that she is in a wheelchair is insignificant. Instead, it is her personality that has attracted him.

Sometimes providing transportation for a date can be a problem. Handicapped individuals who cannot drive can plan ahead and hire a cab, walk a few blocks, or ride a bicycle. If both partners can manipulate wheelchairs, a short ride down the block together can be pleasant. The

point is not to let the mode of transportation hinder a relationship. Where there's a will, there's a way. One alternative is double-dating. A nonhandicapped couple can
pick up the handicapped couple, thus solving a transportation problem. Often with a little foresight, handicapped
people can work things out. Solvable problems should not
stop them from engaging in normal social activities.

Courtship

It is not easy for the handicapped to find privacy while
dating. If their mobility is limited, this makes it even
more difficult. Again, planning is necessary before a date.
If one or the other has difficulty negotiating a wheelchair
or crutches, attending a local movie could be ideal. Most
theaters have street-level entrances that make it easier for
the handicapped person. If he must remain in his wheelchair, some theaters have areas where he can park it and
still see the screen.

Many families today find it acceptable for their teenagers to bring their dates home. Prior arrangement with
the family for use of the living room will insure privacy.
Another convenience is comfortable home furnishings.
This provides more comfort for closeness. Furthermore, it
is fun to take a date out to dinner although this may not
be an easy thing to do. Those who accept themselves and
who are not overly concerned with stares have a fine time.
If they cannot cut up their food, the waiter can help.
There is nothing wrong with asking for such assistance in
a dignified manner. If one partner has difficulty feeding
himself, inviting a close friend along to help him or her
with eating can be the solution. The important thing is
not to forego the pleasure of dining out.

If the couple has many physical obstacles to overcome
in public, the partner can invite the other home for dinner. It would be cozy and friendly. Eating by candlelight
is romantic in courtship. Planning the menu and table de-

cor adds extra pleasure. Whatever the evening's plan is, making sure it is fun and conducive to a comfortable atmosphere is important. Sometimes entertaining at home insures this and is more relaxing and satisfying than trying to contend with theater crowds.

Romance

For any person to have an active sexual life, he must plan and be ready for it. To be attractive to the opposite sex the disabled person must exert himself, and be assertive. He cannot do this by placidly sitting alone, hoping someone will come along. If he is sure of himself he will have no difficulty winking at a woman or giving her an inviting glance. If she responds and he wishes to encourage her, he may choose to invite her to his apartment. He should not let his disability prevent him from exhibiting normal sexual behavior. It is an individual's personality, and not his physical status, that instigates sexual feelings. The fact that he is disabled in some way has no bearing. If he feels attracted to someone he should credit himself with feeling normal. He does himself an injustice if he allows his disability to prevent him from having such feelings and satisfying them. This is healthy and normal behavior.

Institutional Living

Those who are restricted to institutional environments are often sexually repressed. Personnel in these facilities rarely encourage leading a normal existence. The handicapped individual is viewed as a nonsexual human being. He lives in a sterile, isolated environment. Sexual behavior and desires are looked upon with disgust and shame.

Fortunately many nursing homes and residential environments for the handicapped are changing their outlook. They are allowing coed housing. Residences are being built closer to neighborhood resources, therefore encouraging the handicapped to associate more actively with the general public. This allows him to live in as normal an environment as possible. Parties and recreational activities are being encouraged for mixed sexes. Many facilities are setting aside rooms where a couple can socialize privately. These efforts help the disabled person to think of himself as something more than a vegetable, content to lay in bed or fill his time with endless hours sitting in front of a TV. The sexuality of the handicapped should not be dismissed or overlooked because they live in a confined situation. This only results in an individual feeling despondent and frustrated, hence being more difficult to care for.

It is a lot more beneficial to permit sexual normalcy to come to the fore. This is imperative if, in the future, the residents are to move out of the facility and live on their own. Like anyone else, they need to learn self-respect, how to deal with their sexual feelings, and how to be discreet about their behavior. This is necessary if they are to be socially accepted. Any other approach subjects them to criticism and ridicule.

9

WORKING
ENHANCES A PERSON

Being employed helps sustain sexuality in the handicapped individual. When he is unemployed he feels
worthless and nonproductive, and lacks a zest for life.
Many individuals experience these feelings at one time or
another. If their sexuality is developing, these negative
feelings curtail it. If the sexuality is fully developed, negative feelings can repress it. Relating to others becomes
difficult. This can happen to any individual if he cannot
find employment.

The sexuality of the handicapped is affected by the degree of his independence—physical, social, and vocational. In many instances, society does little to help the
disabled person gain his independence. Employers' negative attitudes toward hiring the handicapped add to their
problems. How well the disabled person overcomes the
obstacles determines his future as a productive and sexual
individual. For society to assume that every handicapped
person is unemployable is degrading. The mere act of an
employer taking an inventory of the handicapped's employable skills raises his opinion of himself. He feels there
is some hope for him to make a living. Like other individuals, if the handicapped is employable he should have the
right to work. To deny this is to strip him of dignity.

Fairness is Needed in Social Policy

Many handicapped people find it difficult to secure employment although they know that it is essential they have an income to live on. Some take the easiest way to get this income—they apply for government subsidy checks. This happens especially if the individual has a low self-opinion and thinks of himself as unemployable. He therefore does not make the effort to find a job. He reasons, "Since I am handicapped the government should pay my way." This attitude does little for his social development. However, families also encourage their handicapped offspring to apply for government subsidies. They reason: "He's handicapped, he deserves it, let him have it." In cases where the severity of the handicap makes employment unlikely, these checks are justifiable. In cases where the handicapped person is employable, they only discourage his efforts.

The theory behind government subsidy checks does not encourage the person to work. If he gets a job he is no longer entitled to hospital or medical care that the government provides. This is naturally frightening to a handicapped person. He may have difficulty getting the kind of job that offers these benefits. It would greatly improve things if the government were to allow the handicapped person to at least make a living wage and still receive a disability check. The fear of not being able to make ends meet is alarming and becomes a constant worry. When it is difficult to get a job many wonder what they will do; some hesitate to take a job for fear of losing their government aid.

Robert is an example. He stated, "Why try to get a job? If I work I can only make enough to buy food. If it is more than the government allows I will lose my medical insurance. I am further ahead living on a few of the government's dollars with the assurance that if I am ill I will be able to pay for my medical care." Such government policy lowers the person's self-esteem. He feels he is worthless, even to his country. He would be better served if the government would allow him to earn a poverty-level income before cutting off any assistance. This would allow him to be reasonably self-sufficient. If the individual needs extra assistance to be employable, it should be taken into consideration, e.g., if he needs someone to drive him to his job, he should be able to allot a portion of his government subsidy to cover this expense.

If the handicapped individual does make a substantial income, his government checks should be cut off. However, this should only be done following a careful evaluation of each individual's basic needs to live and work. If he needs personal secretarial help due to his handicap, this need should be granted before cutting off his disability checks. If these factors are implemented into social policy, the tax burden that handicapped people place on this country could be lightened. When they are employed they pay taxes just like everyone else.

The handicapped person needs a job if he is to lead a normal life. Whether it is full-time or part-time makes little difference. Just the fact that he is employed raises his feelings of self-worth. However, the development of such feelings is not possible if he finds he is unable to make enough money to support himself. In this case, he may need the government's help in addition to his earned income. Being employed is much better for him than sitting at home doing nothing and relying on a monthly check from the government. The handicapped will benefit tremendouly if the legislators understand this reasoning and make the effort to rectify the problem.

Many feel that granting the handicapped public welfare is the solution. They argue that this provides a roof over their heads, food in their mouths, and clothes on their backs. Their dignity and their need to be productive is not taken into consideration. As a result, the handicapped person reasons, "Why work? I cannot make enough to live on. When I get older I will be put on welfare." This is the degrading attitude that many handicapped persons live with day after day.

The handicapped person has a right to his dignity and should be granted the chance to provide for himself. He should not have to exist at a lower standard of living than other people. He should have control over his destiny. When he gets a job, he must decide to be productive if he expects business and government to respect him. He should act like a well-adapted, vital person. If he acts fearful and downtrodden, it will be evident to his co-workers. If he rises above his difficulties and strives to do the best he can, others will be conscious of his earnest efforts. However, if the handicapped individual just assumes that he will be secure on welfare, his chances of becoming a vital and productive person lessen; he will be submitting himself to the arbitrary rules and decisions of other people.

The consensus of society is that if a person is handicapped, and unemployed, he is automatically doomed to live a second-class existence on welfare. The case of Peter illustrates this. At twenty-three years of age, he could not walk, had difficulty using his hands, and his speech was unintelligible. Nonetheless, he wanted to make a living. Receiving $110 a month from the government did not stop him from wanting to join the mainstream and work. Finally he found something he could do. A small greeting card company employed him as a salesman and he could work from his home on his own schedule. This seemed ideal for Peter. He entered his new job enthusiastically. He earned a monthly wage of $300. When the local claims office heard of this, they contacted Peter. He was told his subsidy check would be stopped unless he gave up his job. This was grossly unfair. Peter's job gave him a purpose in life and encouraged him to interact with the public. He was faced with the decision to keep working for $300 per month or accept the government subsidy at $110 a month. If he gave up the latter he would lose medical benefits. It was obvious that $300 a month would not support his medical care. Peter was in a dilemma. He was afraid he would not be able to care for himself if he became ill; on the other hand, he was anxious to be employed and productive. When it came time to decide, Peter gave up his job. He went back to living on $110 a month and thus had the assurance that his medical expenses would be paid by the government.

This incident had a profound effect on Peter. He was crushed by having to depend on people to provide his needs. Henceforth, he lost all ambition to look for a job. "What is the use if I cannot keep my government check," he exclaimed. He knew he could not find a job that would pay enough to cover all his expenses. Even though he was physically and educationally limited he wanted to hold a job.

Naturally, it is unrealistic to expect every handicapped person to perform as well as the nonhandicapped on a job. Some do, others do not. This depends on the severity of the physical limitations of the individual. In any case, it is imperative that the federal government consider providing adequate financial support for those handicapped people who have the stamina and willingness to seek employment. It is not fair that they are penalized for having a job.

Rights Under Federal Law Section 504

Since employment is a problem to the handicapped they should be acquainted with federal law Section 504. Many handicapped persons are not familiar with their rights under federal law, and trying to solve a problem without facts is fruitless.

In April, 1977, Joseph A. Califano, Jr., Secretary of

Health, Education, and Welfare, set forth the rights of the handicapped very clearly when he stated:

> Today I am issuing a regulation, pursuant to Section 504 of the Rehabilitation Act of 1973, that will open a new world of equal opportunity for more than 35 million handicapped Americans—the blind, the deaf, persons confined to wheelchairs, the mentally ill or retarded, and those with other handicaps.
> The 504 regulation attacks the discrimination, the demeaning practices and the injustices that have afflicted the nation's handicapped citizens. It reflects the recognition of the Congress that most handicapped persons can lead proud and progressive lives despite their disability. It will usher in a new era of the quality for handicapped individuals in which unfair barriers to self-sufficiency and decent treatment will begin to fall before the force of law. (Statement by Joseph A. Califano, Jr., Secretary of Health, Education, and Welfare on April 28, 1977.)

The handicapped person can take some comfort in the fact that such a federal law now exists. This means he has the right to employment opportunities. Should he wish to work for the federal government he should know that all executive branch agencies must make an annual report to the Civil Service Commission regarding their progress in hiring and promoting disabled persons. In turn, the Civil Service must report to Congress. If a handicapped person believes he has been denied a federal job because of his disability, he should contact the Federal Job Information Center nearest his home. If he feels he has been denied a promotion in a government agency he should contact his Equal Opportunity Employment officer.

Should he not have the right of access to federal buildings, Section 502 sets up a Federal Compliance Board to make sure he has access to all buildings owned, occupied, or financed by the U.S. Government. Section 503 of the law states that firms doing business with the U.S. Government must take action to hire and promote handicapped people. If the person believes his rights have been violated, he should file a complaint within one-hundred-and-twenty days of the alleged violation with Veterans and Handicapped Division, Office of Federal Contract Compliance Programs, Department of Labor, Washington, D.C. 20210.

The Developmental Disability Services and Facilities Construction Act, as amended, also protects the handicapped person. If he is mentally retarded or has cerebral palsy, epilepsy, autism, or dyslexia he is entitled to state legal protection and expanded services as of October, 1977. States were required since that time to have the mechanism to investigate the complaint and take appropriate legal or administrative actions.

For the employable handicapped to be aware of such laws can only help to develop his self-respect and dignity. Fighting the employment problem is no longer his lonely task. The only thing he must do is to act to get a job. No matter what his disability may be, it is now protected by federal law giving him the right to employment.

Getting to the Job

Architectural and transportation barriers are making it more possible for the handicapped to get to a job. In most places this is no longer a problem. There are also plans made to lower housing barriers, so the employed handicapped can live independently. It is being recognized that he does have a right to live privately like everyone else. This allows him to take constructive steps toward leading a normal life. If he merely gives in to feelings of inferiority, self-consciousness, or if he permits his family to brainwash and influence him with their feelings of uncertainty regarding his future, he is relegating himself to a menial lifestyle. He will deprive himself of an opportunity to associate with a co-worker, or share his feelings of success or failure on a job. His sexuality, too, will reach a low ebb. There will be little warmth between him and the rest of humanity.

10

DEVELOPING SEX APPEAL

We live in a society that places a lot of emphasis on appearance. The good grooming of a handicapped person will attract people quicker than how he walks or whether he speaks intelligibly. Being tastefully dressed minimizes his physical characteristics. It enhances his sex appeal. The sloppily dressed and unkempt person, handicapped or not, turns people away.

Fashion is always very much in the news. Well-fitting clothes and prevailing hairstyles are found in magazines and spoken about on radio and television. The handicapped should pay some attention. It should not be difficult for him to meet society's standards. He need not be wealthy to be well-groomed. The only requirement is that the clothes he wears be carefully chosen, kept in good condition, and should reflect his self-esteem.

Parents can help by encouraging their son or daughter to choose the appropriate attire. Making available the latest fashion magazines is one way of doing this. Taking the teenager clothes-shopping is important. The handicapped teenager can benefit from attending a local fashion show. Encouraging a handicapped boy to buy the appropriate shirt or sweater as a gift for a family member will make him aware of the latest fashions. Permitting the handicapped person to be outdated in his attire is damaging to his self-image. He must be encouraged to choose from current fashions.

Having difficulty walking or being confined to a wheel-chair and thus needing assistance to go shopping should not be a reason for the handicapped person to have some-one else choose his clothes. Awareness of sex appeal is stimulated by just going into a department store and choosing for oneself what one thinks will look best. Sex-uality is developed by recognizing individual tastes, just as it is with the nonhandicapped. A shade of lipstick, the color, cut and style of the clothes that one wears should be personally chosen. How we want other people to see us, and how we hope to impress them depend upon what we wear. When this right is denied the handicapped per-son, and when he is kept homebound, he has no way of asserting himself as to how he wishes to appear to others. Often he must content himself with cast-off clothes from siblings or with the choice of clothes colored by the ideas of a parent or another adult.

Body Cleanliness

Sex appeal and the cleanliness of the body are closely related. An individual who looks as if he has not washed for a week or who smells is repulsive. This turns people away and gives them the impression that because he is handicapped, he is not responsible for his personal hy-giene. This is far from the truth. The handicapped should wash himself every day. If he is unable to do so, he should ask for assistance. Bathing indicates that a person cares enough to keep himself clean. Other people will care about him, too. Freshly shampooed hair, the odor of mouthwash on the breath, and the scent of bath powder are not unnoticed by other people. Unshaved armpits and hairy legs are equally offensive. Menstruation periods for handicapped females should be given special attention. If they cannot take care of themselves, they have to ask for assistance. They cannot afford to let themselves be unkempt during menstruation.

The handicapped male should be neatly shaved and should wear a somewhat stylish haircut. This shows that he cares enough about himself to maintain a good self-image. Being alert to contemporary styles helps the disabled person in being more readily accepted by others, which in turn increases his popularity.

Looking Good!

It is important to highlight one's appeal by grooming one's personal appearance. Being careless about this works against one's acceptance by others, as does a gaudy appearance. A medium must be met. If skirts an inch above the knee are in style the handicapped woman may want to consider wearing them. If men are wearing slacks with built-in belts the handicapped man should consider the same. He should make the effort to conform to the current style if possible.

Wearing a well-fitted bra is important for a woman. She will feel better if her undergarments are well-fitting. Sensible shoes are also important. Trying to wear high heels may be unrealistic. If her stockings have runs in them, she will appear sloppy. Her unkempt appearance will be attributed to her handicap. She should guard against such assumptions. She cannot afford to have other people making snap judgements about her.

It is not different at all for the handicapped man. It pays off for the handicapped man to take a minute to check whether his clothing is soiled. Well-pressed slacks and shiny shoes give a neat appearance and add to his attractiveness. If his colors match he will appear well-groomed. It isn't enough to only cover the body. How clothes look on the body is important as well.

The health of the handicapped person's sexuality is influenced by how others regard him. His appearance plays an important part; this includes the quality and condition of the equipment he uses to function. A wheelchair that squeaks and is falling apart, or crutches that need to be revarnished, do not help to project a good appearance. Should he be bedridden, clean sheets and brightly-colored blankets and bedspreads make him feel better about himself, and he is more acceptable to those around him.

Commercial Toiletries

Medical items should not be the only drugstore purchase for the handicapped. Cologne, bath oils, deodorant, makeup, aftershave lotion, douches, and mouthwash should be a part of his everyday care. Ignoring these necessities does not enhance his sex appeal. The handicapped person should want to look and feel sexy. The right shade of lipstick, a dab of rouge, and a touch of mascara to the eyelashes can do much to develop a welcome look. Wearing a gold necklace indicates, today, that a man is in fashion. Failure to catch on to these items of sex appeal may result in the handicapped person appearing as a nonsocial, asexual being.

Good Health is Vital

Everyone should have an annual physical checkup. Being handicapped is no exception to this rule. For instance, cancer, heart diseases, or diabetes are nondiscriminatory. Diseases can afflict the able, as well as the disabled, body. Prostate gland problems can occur as frequently in handicapped as in nonhandicapped men. The need to periodically check for breast cancer or suspicious tumors should not be overlooked. Gynecological checkups are essential to every female. The handicapped person himself or someone taking care of him should be on the lookout for any abnormalities.

Good dental care is an important health habit. Should the handicapped person have pronounced facial grimaces, his teeth should be in good shape. This makes his facial expression less objectionable. Good teeth also insure the chewing of food and therefore good digestion. The same care applies to vision. If corrective glasses are needed, the individual should wear them. Eyes should be checked by age three, unless a problem is detected earlier.

One's overall health has an undeniable relationship with one's social and sexual performance. Contrary to what many assume, most handicapped people can be in good health. However, as with anyone else, he must take good care of himself. If he doesn't, he is bound to have health problems. One way of avoiding this is for the handicapped person to keep abreast of the handicapping condition. The individual and his family should be continuously aware of the need for braces, medication, or any other special equipment. A yearly checkup is advisable for young and old. In this age of medical advances the handicapped person and his family should avail themselves of all the latest medical breakthroughs. His active interest in his own well-being is helpful in maintaining his self-esteem.

Diet is Important

Being overweight is a common problem. If the handicapped person cannot move about easily or exercise much, having excess weight compounds his problem and is detrimental to his body's circulatory system. This condition is especially dangerous to those confined to a bed or a wheelchair. When the handicapped person cares about his health and body, it indicates that he accepts the responsibility for his own welfare. Moreover, the overweight handicapped person is a burden to those who must lift and care for him. A daily program of physical exercise is essential.

A face with pimples or acne is unattractive. If it is the result of poor diet or unclean skin, it should be rectified. The method used is up to the individual. It may be necessary to consult the family physician. Or it may require self-discipline in not overeating. Whatever the cause, precaution should be taken to minimize skin problems.

Questionable Vices

Drinking occasionally is acceptable. However, for the handicapped person to give in to a regular diet of alcohol because it makes him feel good can lead to social, and sexual, problems. His drinking habit can make him socially unacceptable. Having a cocktail to enjoy, rather than to escape, is permissible if done in moderation. If the person is on any medication, he should consult his doctor before indulging. He is being totally unrealistic if he thinks that several drinks will minimize his handicap and its associated problems. When the effects of drink wear off, the problems are still there.

The idea that alcohol acts as a relaxant for some physical handicaps is incorrect. In many cases it merely causes the individual to lose what control he might otherwise have over his body. It can cause very tense muscles, spasms, and slurred speech. For this reason it is unwise, and borders on meanness, when the able-bodied person encourages the handicapped, "Here, have a drink, it will relax you and you will do better." Handicapped persons themselves often fall into this delusion when they drink. Unless they understand the true nature of drinking it can quickly become a habit-forming escape from their condition.

Smoking can be as hazardous to health as drinking. If the reason for smoking is to try to cope with nervousness or boredom, finding an interesting alternative such as needlework or playing electronic games can be helpful. To plan to set aside money that would be spent on cigarettes for some long-yearned-for item is a good idea. For those who must smoke, pick low-tar cigarettes.

·11·

FALLING IN LOVE

Physical techniques for engaging in sexual activities in an intimate relationship will be explained in a sequel to this book. This chapter discusses the nature of lovemaking, what it is, how it can be accomplished. It is applicable to dating or engaged partners, and to married couples. Those considering a long-term relationship should be knowledgeable about the factors involved. The lack of such knowledge can result in unhappiness, frustration, and misunderstanding between two people.

Earlier chapters have emphasized the psychological preparation the handicapped individual must make if he is to love another person. If he is now at the point where he can make another person happy he is probably ready to make love. He will enjoy the human warmth of giving and receiving. He will tingle with the excitement of anticipation and will want to relate intimately to a partner. If the emotional exchange feels right, the other partner will also be motivated to give of himself or herself. As a result, they will mutually feel satisfied and close to each other. In this euphoric state the physical handicap fades into the background. The body relaxes; life takes on new meaning. Feelings of loneliness subside and that of togetherness grow. The individual is sensitive to the needs and feelings of his or her partner. There is no longer the reason for

self-centeredness. Intelligible speech is no longer necessary. The tone of voice, and the right time and place are
important factors. Regardless of how unintelligible they
are, words spoken in an affectionate manner can arouse
tenderness. When one's love is intense for one's partner,
the importance of a scarred face or distorted facial expressions become minimized. All efforts center instead around
satisfying and pleasing one's lover.

Setting the Stage

Choosing an enticing atmosphere for lovemaking cannot
be overlooked. Soft music and dim lights are romantic
touches. Privacy is essential. Without it the partners
would not be relaxed. To act and speak freely to another
about the way one feels is important.

The atmosphere that is created will depend upon the
couple involved. If they are both in wheelchairs, perhaps
staying at one or the other's home for the evening is the
answer. If the couple is fortunate enough and can get
around unassisted, they may prefer going to a nearby
park. The couple needs to respect each other's dignity in
their lovemaking. Due to the prevailing public misconception that the handicapped person is sexless, he should
be discreet in demonstrating affection. Both partners
should be aware of this if they are to enjoy their relationship to its fullest extent, without undue external stress.

Pleasure in Touching

The human body always responds to touch. The infant
snuggles deep in his mother's arms as she strokes his
body. When partners touch, warm feelings surge through
them. This physical contentment can be experienced by
the handicapped person. Poor physical coordination, weak
limbs, or stiff arms and hands should not be barriers. The
fundamental point is that body contact is in itself pleasurable. This may seem strange and new to some handi-

capped people because they lack an understanding of the sensation they feel. They have been deprived of human touch and must learn to enjoy it. They must become acquainted with intimate warmth as compared to the impersonal handling they experience in clinical settings. They must learn that touching another person is a form of communicating love. Their sense of touch has to be developed and they must also learn how to react to it.

Some handicaps cause severe body tension. However, this can be reduced by a partner's gentle touch; if a feeling of love exists it is soothing. In the case of cerebral palsy this has proved true. Where poor body coordination exists, efforts to please a partner improve coordination. When the individual concentrates on giving pleasure to his loved one, his handicapping side effects often are minimized. At this point he feels warm and secure as lovemaking progresses. The worry about performance subsides as he focuses on pleasing his partner. Mutual stroking and touching arouse sexual feelings and the couple enters a world of tranquil pleasure. The poorly coordinated hand, when stroking the partner's body, becomes more controllable. In some instances such gestures might be regarded as rough. However, they are gentle in this act because the handicapped person is not afraid to express his feelings.

The motion of stroking the head, neck, arms, and legs should be as normal for the handicapped as it is for the nonhandicapped. This is the way to get to know another's body. Sexual happiness results when each partner can stimulate the other to orgasm. Rather than look upon this with fear and disgust it is important to realize that the relationship is growing more intimate. Only a few handicaps prevent this from happening. Otherwise, it is a perfectly normal occurrence in lovemaking. Emotions and sexual feelings are not dead in the handicapped person, contrary to popular belief. Not to recognize this does the handicapped an injustice: it relegates him to an unnatural, nonsexual status.

Lovemaking

Sometimes the severity of a handicap makes it difficult to engage in lovemaking. However, persons with this problem should not despair. By having someone put them on a floor mat next to each other provides the opportunity for experimentation. Satisfaction can be gained by lying close to one another. If the movement of the upper limbs is limited, just touching the arm of the partner is better than nothing at all. Perhaps their legs can be pressed together. Regardless of how limited the activity, it can be quite satisfying. They should not be deprived altogether of the enjoyment of being together. If those who aid them accept the need for and the normalcy of this setup, they are providing the conditions conducive to the partners' expression of affection. Leaving the couple alone and checking in occasionally to see if they need assistance or repositioning is also helpful.

If one partner can speak intelligibly, but cannot write, he might want to tape his feelings for his partner. His partner will be thrilled to listen to his voice and words. Asking a family member or close friend to buy flowers is another way to express love.

Some handicapped couples may find it difficult to have easy access to each other's body. This can be remedied by putting swimming trunks on the man and a bathing suit on the woman, thus allowing more body area to be exposed and touched. Lying on a mat in the warm sunshine or in front of a fire is a good time for the couple to explore each other's body. The partner's touch can suffice and be an adequate substitute for sexual intercourse. Usually, the partners will know the limits of their sexual behavior and will try to get ample physical satisfaction under the circumstances. All they need is the opportunity to express themselves. Whether a third person is necessary to consummate the sexual act is a decision for individual couples to make. Some may not wish to have a third person around. They may find their limited techniques satisfying enough. Their goal is to make each other happy and to enjoy their interaction.

Expressing Sexual Desires

If a disabled person has special difficulty expressing sexual feelings, he should not give up. Instead, he should familiarize himself with his physical limitations and discuss them with his partner. When both understand the problems that may arise and mutually find ways to minimize them, there will be no serious block to the relationship. If holding hands is too basic, perhaps rubbing shoulders and arms, or licking and sucking the other's skin, can be satisfying. Sitting cheek to cheek and hugging are other ways. Rubbing each other's noses and running the hands through the hair can be stimulating. If the feet and legs are better coordinated than the arms and hands, kicking off the shoes and socks and playing with each other's feet can be very enjoyable.

Each partner should be aware of the other's preferences. To try and satisfy only personal needs is simply selfish and can lead to misunderstanding, frustration, and ultimately the breakup of the relationship. In fact, healthy sexuality is a boost to the ego. This happened in the case of Cathy and Joe.

When they developed a sexual bond it broke the boredom and hopelessness of their lives and strengthened their will to live. They fought their way out of their individual isolation and created the conditions that made it possible for them to live in the outside world. By pooling their resources of physical abilities and willpower, they managed to cope together. No one looked upon their relationship in disgust. Had this happened it would have been a most degrading experience for them and might have resulted in deep, lasting depressions.

Masturbation

Everyone masturbates sometime in their lives. Therefore, it is normal for the handicapped to masturbate. It is important to know that it does not jeopardize one's health or well-being. On the contrary, psychological problems can result if it is looked upon as abnormal. Guilt complexes and feelings of anxiety will manifest themselves. Ironically, the behavior may become more frequent. Masturbation is one aspect of the transitional phase from early childhood to adulthood. It is a valid means for an individual to get to know himself, his body, and his sexual needs. Moreover, in the case of the handicapped person, it is sometimes the only technique to satisfy one's sexual feelings.

Restless feelings in the handicapped person cannot be underestimated; they arise in him as in anyone else. He often becomes overpowered by sudden floods of sexual feelings and strong bodily sensations. A potent fear of handicapped men and women is that they will not have the opportunity to be sexually active and/or love another person. This is a devastating and debilitating feeling. For the handicapped person to resign himself to the fact that he may never have a relationship will not reduce his vital sexual needs. Helping him choose an acceptable time and place to satisfy sexual urges is essential. It is the handicapped person's private affair. There is nothing wrong with it. It only becomes a problem when he masturbates publicly which leaves him susceptible to social condemnation.

Mutual masturbation may be the sole technique that a handicapped couple can use for sexual satisfaction. Too much tenseness in the genital area or tense arms and hands may prevent total sexual fulfillment. Some handicapped couples may have to employ special aids such as a lubricant jelly to make touching more pleasurable. Putting on a bath mitt is another method to make a shaky hand gentle, or putting warm water in a spray bottle and spraying the partner's genital area can cause excitement. Just the fact that these things are done by the partner is sexually arousing. Vibrators and hand-held shower massagers are other methods that can be employed by those who are capable of using them without injury to the body. In all these instances, the primary goal is for the individuals to learn to use and enjoy sexually arousing techniques. The important thing is that the handicapped person engage in those activities which he can master. Under no circumstances should sexuality be dismissed because of a handicap.

Is Sexual Intercourse Necessary?

For the severely disabled to consummate the sex act by intercourse may be out of the question. However, such a couple should not despair. If they understand beforehand what their sexual activity will involve, they can determine the outcome of their relationship. Perhaps the lovers will decide that their marriage should be without sex or with only limited sexual activity. The important thing is for them to agree on an arrangement. When the handicap dictates that normal sexual behavior is out of the question the well-adjusted couple makes allowances for the situation.

Marriage

The ultimate goal for most couples in love is marriage. This is also true for the handicapped. However, the handicapped couple may have other things to take into account prior to a marriage commitment. For instance, are they able financially to support themselves? Can they function without their family to help them financially? Questions such as these must be realistically answered before marriage can be considered. It is unwise to burden family members with these problems. For a couple to do this to satisfy their wish to marry is selfish.

Another important consideration is whether or not to have children. If both partners require a lot of assistance, to have children may be unwise. Serious thought should be given to the psychological effects handicapped parents can have on a child. Special attention should be given to whether they can provide safe care for an infant. Are they capable of rendering medical care in the event of an emergency? Can they warn the child of dangers? Will the child develop limited social contacts because his parents cannot take him places? These questions that are related to the child's welfare must be answered before parenting. To give birth to a child just to prove one's womanliness or manliness is detrimental to all concerned. To pass on the raising of the child to in-laws or close relatives because it will be easier or safer is not the solution. Again, the couple needs to consider the pros and cons of parenting prior to marriage.

If the couple is able to take care of themselves, and their child, raising a child may not be a problem. However, they should keep in mind that such an undertaking involves stress, time, and money. The parents should be well-adjusted individuals so they can show as much love and interest to the child as is required. Emphasis should be placed on making every effort so that he lives as normal a life as possible. There is no room to feel sad because of their handicaps. They should not burden their child with their problems for this could result in the child feeling unhappy, ridiculed, and rejected by his friends. The same can be true if only one parent is handicapped.

Abortion
The author feels that the matter of abortion should be left up to the individual. If a handicapped woman considers abortion it should be a private decision. It should not

depend on the attitudes of her friends or family. The fact that she is handicapped should not make any difference. If she has religious and personal convictions, these may affect her decision. If she cannot make a decision she is comfortable with, she should seek professional help. While she may seek the advice of those around her, she should not necessarily submit to their opinions.

Sterilization

If the handicapped person is of sound intelligence and reason his investigation into the matter of sterilization should be thorough. Careful consideration of all the factors that warrant sterilization is important. Ill health may make it unadvisable for a woman to have children. If a couple chooses a lifestyle without children, sterilization could be the answer. For the handicapped person to submit to a sterilization operation to please his parents is to jeopardize his rights as an individual. If the individual is able to reason for himself, hopefully, those around him will respect him enough to allow him to make his own decision. Arbitrarily insisting that he should be sterilized is to unfairly manipulate another person's future. His handicap does not give anyone the right to do so.

Homosexuality

The sexual preference of a man or woman should be their personal choice. Even so, the subject of homosexuality is very controversial today. As with any other minority group, the gay population is trying to validate their existence. Different areas of the country differ in their acceptance of homosexuality. It seems that on the West Coast it is more accepted than other regions of the country. Some religions tolerate gay people; others vehemently oppose them. In spite of this some gays are militant in their efforts for acceptance; others are quiet and passive. In some places gay people are a potent political force. On the whole, this appears to continue to be a burgeoning social movement.

An individual's sexual preference should be exclusively his own decision. This applies to the handicapped as well. He should consider his options and the problems he would encounter. In view of the handicapped's present social status, the handicapped person should not be too quick to lend support to this group on a militant basis. Being disabled, the handicapped person already has one strike against him; to join a group that is not socially accepted can only add to his dilemma. This is not, however, to advise him to act one way or the other. It is merely to point out that he can encounter additional problems that his nonhandicapped peers do not. Generally, for the handicapped to engage in any kind of conspicuous behavior underscores his condition. This applies not only to sexual choice but also to any public involvement with controversial subjects.

There are those who believe that choosing the alternate lifestyle of homsexuality is a sexual solution for the handicapped. This is a matter of opinion. The handicapped person should be cognizant of all the problems that might occur. Is he willing to be conspicuous, even more so than his handicap has made him? Is he willing to have his nonhandicapped peers reject him because he chose to publicly join a marginal social group?

These are questions the handicapped person should ask himself. His answers will help him determine his sexual preference. Like any other person, the handicapped person owes himself the right to make careful decisions that may affect him mentally, socially, emotionally, and sexually. Once these questions are answered and decisions are reached, he is free to exercise his sexual choice.

A HOPEFUL FUTURE

M ainstreaming the handicapped into society helps develop his sexuality. Instead of being considered different, he will be accepted as a vital, functioning individual. The only difference between him and others is that he has specific limitations. More and more people are seeing him in this light. Society, however, plays an important role in helping to assure that a relaxed integration takes place between the handicapped and nonhandicapped. This encourages the disabled person to work and live comfortably. When this socialization takes place sporadically, it implies that the handicapped is unequal in the eyes of his fellow man. It should be realized that he can develop a strong, healthy self-image if his perceptions are based on a genuine understanding of himself and others. This occurs when he associates with the nonhandicapped. It will not occur if people continue to be prejudiced toward the handicapped person.

Disabled children who are part of the mainstream in an educational setting will find socialization much easier as they grow older. This allows them at a young age to learn to associate with nonhandicapped peers. Continuation of this is essential if the next generation of handicapped people is to live and work among the nonhandicapped. For those who are brought up in segregated educational environments, this will be more difficult. They will have to work harder to make the adjustment. However, they should not despair for it is their birthright that they are striving for. It may be blocked from time to time by those who misunderstand them, yet a continuous effort to attain full status must be pursued.

The handicapped person and his family can also do much to aid in their educational and social integration, and their employment opportunity. Society can help make resources available to them; however, the rest is up to the handicapped individual. Only when he is willing to join the mainstream and swallow his fears will the handicapped person become a part of society. Obviously this cannot be done by sitting at home. It requires the handicapped person's not fearing to take the risk of involving himself in the mainstream and striving to make the adjustments.

Attitudes Must Change

The effort needed is twofold. Society must change and the handicapped person must change. One cannot without the help of the other. Society must be educated on how it can change to help the handicapped feel more at ease and more vital, and to feel wanted and worthwhile. This process takes time. However, when society views the handicapped person as a social, sexual, vital individual regardless of his limitations, he will be halfway there. The same is true for the handicapped. If they view society as a challenge they want to experience and contribute to, there will be a meeting of needs and purposes.

Opening Doors into Society

Segregating the handicapped hinders the growth of their sexuality. Where the handicapped person lives should not be determined by his physical disability. He should have the same right as anyone else to live where he wishes. Efforts should be made to set up residences in an acceptable, safe part of the community. Where the handicapped live is as important an issue for them as it is for the nonhandicapped.

A case in point is a recent residential program that has been developed in a midwestern city. Although the physical layout for the program is modern and is equipped with necessary conveniences, its location is in a rundown neighborhood in the city. One thinks twice before visiting the facility after dark. As a result, the residents are confined to their apartments until they can be escorted by someone who can look out for their safety. Had this residential program been located in a neighborhood that had a lower crime rate, they could go out by themselves and be more independent. Many of the residents feel they were given a place to live in a rundown section of the city because they were considered second-class citizens. When they spoke about this, they were told there was no other place to put them. Yet, a new high school was being built five blocks away in a safe neighborhood. The handicapped people felt they did not rate. It was degrading to them and they felt worthless.

Begging for Pity is Over

There are many expenses involved in being handicapped. Some of these must be met by the individual or his family; others are assumed by society. In both cases money must be raised. How this is done has a bearing on how one regards the handicapped person: if it is done in a condescending manner he will feel degraded, i.e., as if he were a burden to everyone.

The mere act of collecting dollars for the handicapped labels them as subservient individuals. People feel they are contributing to the poor, the helpless, or the ill. Rarely do they feel that they may be collecting money for worthwhile people who can provide for their own needs.

The handicapped person should not be looked upon as someone to whom others must cater. This is demeaning. If money were collected for a general health service fund to be broken down later for each humanitarian need, it would be less stigmatizing. If there was a telethon for a general health service fund to be broken down later for each serious illness, i.e. cerebral palsy, cancer, heart disease, muscular dystrophy, it would be less stigmatizing. This would deemphasize the pity and sense of helplessness placed on the physically handicapped in telethons today, and emphasize instead the general funding need for all handicaps. Collecting money for the needy helps some people feel good about themselves. It assures them that they are not as bad off as the crippled man in the street, or the lady in the wheelchair seen at the supermarket. At the expense of someone else's misfortune they feed their own image. It gives them a good reputation in their community and makes them feel worthwhile.

Telethons create a negative concept of the handicapped. One switch of the TV dial and the handicapped individual appears on the home screen whether he is wanted or not. Imposing on the public does little to improve the status of the handicapped. Telethon organizers have become too cunning and sophisticated in manipulating the public. They try to wring every last tear of pity, every bit of guilt, and every penny from the sympathetic viewer. Rather than giving the idea that the handicapped is a worthwhile group, the audience is left with the idea that the only thing handicapped people want is their money and pity. Nevertheless, telethons persist year in and year out. Although some of the money collected go toward research, a greater portion goes to promoters, managers, administrators, and professional fundraisers. It should not be overlooked that telethons are big business and showcases for people who promote their interests in others for their own purposes.

To raise funds, telethons have a tendency to exploit the handicapped. Those running the program inadvertently make the handicapped individual feel he is indispensable to the success of the show. They encourage him to display his helplessness, hoping the TV viewers will give money out of pity for the handicapped person. This gives the disabled young person a false concept of himself. Rarely does he understand that the audience is pitying him rather than being entertained by his performance. He gets the idea that everyone wants to see him on television. Little does he realize that the minute he pathetically appears many people change channels or turn off their TVs. They can't stand to watch him.

Telethons tend to present handicapped people as loners who constantly dwell on their handicaps. They are presented in a dehumanized way; they do not grow, play, or aspire to goals. They are burdens, not contributing members to their families. This will be the case if the disabled person continues to be categorized as "different." Society will continue to neglect his needs by giving him lower priority than other people. They will continue to be placed in separate, out-of-the-way hospitals and institutions and they will continue to be treated as an object of charity rather than as an equal human being.

People frequently determine their own intelligence, appearance, productiveness, and personal worth through a process of learning. The disabled person is no different. If professionals believe his disability can be overcome, the individual will also believe it. If the attitude is that nothing can be done, only a strong-willed person will keep trying. A falsely high hope may lead to premature defeat. These attitudes are particularly influential when they are in the hands of those who make critical decisions about the handicapped person's life. Parents, teachers, doctors, and employers should be cautious in this respect.

The Outlook is Positive

Steps toward equality for the handicapped person are being taken in education, rehabilitation, employment, housing, transportation, and civil rights. People are beginning to appreciate the fact that there does exist among the handicapped a vast resource of untapped energy, creativity, vision, productivity, potential, and power. Society is beginning to see that it is within their capacity to use their resources, slowly and carefully at first, but surely and steadfastly, on behalf of the handicapped population. People are starting to understand that disabling conditions are sometimes aggravated by society itself. They are beginning to realize that by freeing real abilities from the shackles of disabilities they are rehabilitating not only disabled people but society as well.

When the disabled person becomes a vital, social, and sexual individual he will raise the consciousness of people around him. They will acknowledge his needs, problems, and concerns. Ultimately, this is what is needed. The handicapped person does not necessarily need charity or to live on welfare, nor does he need to exist in a perpetual childhood. What he needs is the opportunity to develop and apply his social and sexual abilities to his fullest potential. This will happen when business and professional circles recognize the contributions of the handicapped worker. It will happen when educators perceive instruction as more of a matter of encouraging strengths than one of giving in to weaknesses. It will happen when lawmakers conceive laws not to pacify disabled activists with empty words but to solve problems with enforceable requirements. In the end, it will happen when the average citizen looks at a woman in a wheelchair or a man on crutches, not as people who can't, but as people who can—seeing not the chrome, wires, and wood so much as the individual and unique qualities that make him human.

APPENDIX I

Selected Bibliography

Ayrault, Evelyn West. *Growing Up Handicapped.* New York: The Continuum Publishing Corporation, 1977.

———. *Helping the Handicapped Teenager Mature.* New York: Associated Press, 1971.

———. *Take One Step.* New York: Doubleday & Company, Inc., 1963.

Blanton, Smiley, M.D., *Love or Perish.* New York: Fawcett World Library, 1955, 1956.

Bowe, Frank G., *Handicapping America: Barriers to Disabled People.* New York: Harper & Row, Publishers, Inc., 1978.

Doniger, Simon, *Becoming the Complete Adult.* New York: Associated Press, 1962.

Downing, George, *The Massage Book.* New York: Random House, 1972.

Enby, Gunnel, *Let There Be Love.* New York: Taplinger Publishing Company, 1972.

Friday, Nancy, *My Mother, My Self.* New York: Delacorte Press, 1977.

———. *Men In Love.* New York: Delacorte Press, 1980.

Fromm, Erich, *The Art of Loving.* New York: Harper & Row Publishers, Inc., 1956.

Fromme, Allan, *The Ability to Love.* New York: Farrar, Straus & Giroux, 1963, 1965.

Gadpaille, Warren J., M.D., *The Cycles of Sex.* New York: Charles Scribner's Sons, 1975.

Gordon, Sol, *Facts About Sex for Today's Youth.* Rev. Ed. New York: John Day, 1973.

———. *Let's Make Sex a Household Word.* New York: John Day, 1975.

———. *Living Fully: A Guide for Young People with a Handicap, Their Parents, Their Teachers, & Professionals.* New York: John Day, 1975.

Hamilton, Eleanor, Ph.D., *Sex, with Love, A Guide for Young People.* Boston: Beacon Press, 1978.

Heslinga, K., Ph.D., Schellen, A. M. C., M.D., and Verkuyl, A., M.D., *Not Made of Stone.* Springfield, Illinois: Charles C. Thomas Publishers, 1974.

Hopper, C. Edmund, M. Ed., and Allen, William A., M.P.H., *Sex Education for the Physically Handicapped Youth* Springfield, Illinois: Charles C. Thomas Publisher's, 1980.

Hunt, Morton, *Gay.* New York: Farrar, Straus & Giroux, Inc., 1977.

Johnson, Warren R., Ed.D., *Sex Education and Counseling of Special Groups.* Springfield, Illinois: Charles C. Thomas Publishers, 1975.

Lancaster-Gaye, Derek, *Personal Relationships, the Handicapped and the Community.* London and Boston: Routledge & Kegan Paul, 1972.

Lowen, Alexander, M.D., *The Betrayal of the Body.* New York: Collier Books, 1967.

————. *Pleasure: A Creative Approach to Life.* New York: Penguin Books, 1975.

Marinelli, Robert P., and Dell Orto, Arthur E., eds., *The Psychology and Social Impact of Physical Disability.* New York: Springer Publishing Company, 1977.

Maslow, Abraham H., *Toward a Psychology of Being.* New York: D. Van Nostrand Company, 1968.

Peale, Norman Vincent, D.D., and Blanton, Smiley, M.D. *The Art of Real Happiness.* Greenwich, Connecticut: Fawcett Publications, 1950, 1956.

Peale, Norman Vincent, D.D. *The Power of Positive Thinking.* New York: Fawcett Crest, 1952, 1956.

Robinault, Isabel P., *Sex, Society, and the Disabled.* New York: Harper & Row, 1978.

Rogers, Carl R., *On Becoming a Person.* Boston: Houghton Mifflin Company, 1961.

————. *Carl Rogers on Encounter Groups.* New York: Harper & Row, Publishers, Inc., 1970.

Sheehy, Gail, *Passages.* New York: E. P. Dutton, 1974.

Vermes, Hal G., *The Boy's Book of Personal Development.* New York: Association Press, 1964.

Vermes, Jean C., *The Girl's Book of Personal Development.* New York: Association Press, 1964.

Wright, Beatrice A., *Physical Disability—A Psychological Approach.* New York: Harper & Row, Publishers, Inc., 1960.

APPENDIX II

Some Terms Associated with Handicapped People *

Amputation

Removal, usually by surgery, of a limb, part, or organ. Amputation of parts of the fetus in utero, formerly believed to be caused by constricting bands but now believed to be a developmental defect.

Amyotonia Congenital

Deficiency or lack of muscular tone. A noninherited but sometimes familial disease characterized by absence of muscular development, with the lower extremities being the first involved. It is first seen at, or shortly after, birth.

Arthritis

Inflammation of a joint, usually accompanied by pain and, frequently, changes in structure. Arthritis may result from, or be associated with, a number of conditions including: infection (gonococcal, tuberculous, pneumococcal); rheumatic fever; ulcerative colitis; trauma; neurogenic disturbances as tabes dorsalis; degenerative joint disease as osteoarthritis; metabolic disturbances as gout; neoplasms as synovioma; hydrarthrosis; para- or periarticular conditions as fibromyositis, myositis, or bursitis;

* From *Taber's Cyclopedic Medical Dictionary.* 14th ed. Edited by Clayton L. Thomas. Philadelphia: F. A. Davis Co., 1981. Reprinted by permission.

various other conditions as acromegaly, psoriasis, Raynaud's disease.

1. *Osteo-arthritis;* A chronic disease involving the joints, especially those bearing weight. Characterized by degeneration of articular cartilage, overgrowth of bone with lipping and spur formation, and impaired function.

2. *Rheumatoid arthritis:* A chronic systemic disease characterized by inflammatory changes in joints and related structures that result in crippling deformities. The specific cause is unknown but it is generally believed that the pathological changes in the joints are related to an antigen–antibody reaction which is poorly understood. Environmental and familial factors are of doubtful importance. Onset may vary, but usually occurs in middle age.

Cerebral Palsy

Bilateral, symmetrical, nonprogressive paralysis resulting from developmental defects in brain or trauma at birth. Temporary or permanent loss of sensation or loss of ability to move or to control movement. Palsy arising from an injury received at birth.

1. *Ataxia:* Failure or irregularity of muscular coordination, especially that manifested when voluntary muscular movements are attempted.

2. *Athetosis:* A condition wherein there are slow, irregular, twisting, snakelike movements seen in the upper extremities, especially in the hands and fingers, and performed involuntarily. The symptoms may be due to one of several diseases, including encephalitis and tabes dorsalis.

3. *Rigidity:* a. Tenseness; immovability; stiffness; inability to bend or be bent. b. In psychiatry, refers to one who is excessively resistant to change. c. Cerebellar: Stiffness of body and extremities resulting from lesion of middle lobe of cerebellum. d. Cogwheel: Condition noted upon passively stretching a hypertonic muscle in which resistance is jerky. e. Decerebrate: Sustained contraction of extensor muscles of limbs resulting from a lesion in the brain stem between superior colliculi and vestibular nuclei.

4. *Spastic:* a. Resembling or of the nature of spasms or convul-

sions. b. Produced by spasms. c. Spastic gait—a stiff movement with toes seeming to catch together and to drag. d. Spastic paralysis—Muscular rigidity accompanying partial paralysis. Usually due to a lesion involving upper motor neurons. e. Spasticity—Increased tone or contractions of muscles causing stiff and awkward movements: the result of upper motor neuron lesion.

5. *Tremor:* a. A quivering, especially continuous quivering of a convulsive nature. b. An involuntary movement of a part or parts of the body resulting from alternate contractions of opposing muscles. Tremors may be classified as involuntary, static, dynamic, kinetic, hereditary, and hysteric. Pathologic tremors are independent of the will. The trembling may be fine or coarse, rapid or slow; may appear on movement (intention tremor) or improve when the part is employed. Often due to organic disease, trembling may express an emotion (e.g., fear). c. Muscular: Slight oscillating muscular contractions in rhythmical order.

Congenital Dislocation of the Hip
Present at birth. Causes: 1. Hereditary. 2. A local vascular or metabolic disturbance in early life of embryo. 3. Pressure that brings about prolonged malposition which can result in a stretching and lengthening of the ligaments in the hip joint.

Disability
Lack of ability to perform mental or physical tasks which one can normally do. The term is used in legal medicine to apply especially to the loss of mental or physical powers as a result of injury or disease.

Encephalitis
Inflammation of the brain. It may be a specific disease entity caused by an arthropod-borne (*arbor*) virus, or it may occur as a sequela of influenza, measles, German measles, chicken pox, smallpox, vaccinia, or other diseases.

1. *Infantile:* Brain inflammation in the young which may cause cerebral palsy.
2. *Lethargica:* A disease of the nervous system thought to be

caused by a virus. Characterized by lethargy, oculomotor paralysis, clonic and choreiform movements, rigidity, delirium, stupor, coma, and reversal of sleep rhythm. The disease first appeared pandemically in 1916 to 1917, and is now considered extinct.
3. *Periaxialis:* Inflammation of the white matter of the cerebrum, occuring mainly in the young.

Handicap

A mental or physical impairment which prevents or interferes with normal mental or physical activities and achievement. All living organisms have as a basic characteristic being able to adapt to handicaps. This is particularly true of human beings, some of whom are able to live useful, rewarding, and satisfying lives despite multiple handicaps.

Intelligence

The capacity to comprehend relationships. The ability to think, to solve problems, and to adjust to new situations. It is doubtful that using a single test to estimate the intelligence of persons from different social, racial, cultural, or economic backgrounds is reliable.
1. Quotient: An index of relative intelligence determined through the subject's answers to arbitrarily chosen questions. Intelligence quotient is merely a standard score which places an individual in reference to the scores of others within his age group. Abbreviation: IQ.
2. Test: A test designed to determine the intelligence of an individual. A number of tests have been devised including the Binet, Babcock–Levy, and Stanford–Binet tests. Tests are used as a basis for determining intelligence quotient (IQ).
3. Classification of IQ:

IQ	*Classification*
Above 140	Near genius or genius
120—140	Very superior intelligence
110—120	Superior intelligence
90—110	Normal or average intelligence
80—90	Dull Normal

70—80	Borderline deficiency
50—70	Educable mentally retarded
30—50	Trainable
20—30	Profoundly mentally retarded

Love
1. Concern and affection for another person. This may be to such a degree as to cause individuals to risk losing their lives in their concern for the safety, care, and well-being of another. 2. In psychiatry, love is equated to pleasure, particularly as it applies to the gratifying sexual experiences between individuals.

Meningitis
Inflammation of the membranes of the spinal cord or brain.
1. Cerebral: Acute or chronic meningitis of the brain.
2. Cerebrospinal: Meningitis of brain and spinal cord.
3. Spinal: Meningitis of spinal cord membranes.
4. Traumatic: Meningitis resulting from traumatism or injury.

Mental Age
Age of a person with respect to the intellectual development as contrasted with the chronological age.

Mental Retardation
Deficient intellectual development. Levels of mental retardation according to IQ score ranges are:

> Borderline: 70—80
> Mild: 52—69
> Moderate: 36—54
> Severe: 20—39
> Profound: 19 and below

Mentality
Mental power or activity.

Multiple sclerosis
A chronic, slowly progressive disease of the central nervous system characterized by development of disseminated demyeliated glial patches called plaques. Symptoms and signs are numerous,

but in later stages those of charcot's triad (nystagmus, scanning speech, and intention tremor) are common. Occurs in the form of many clinical syndromes, the most common being the cerebral, brain stem–cerebellar, and spinal. A history of remissions and exacerbations is diagnostic. Etiology is unknown and there is no specific therapy.

Muscular Dystrophy

Wasting away and atrophy of muscles. 1. Dystrophy—disorder caused by defective nutrition or metabolism. 2. Progressive muscular—a familial disease characterized by progressive atrophy and wasting of muscles. Onset is usually at an early age and it occurs more frequently in males than females. Its cause is thought to be a genetic defect in muscle metabolism.

Myasthenia

Muscular weakness. Gravis Myasthenia is a disease characterized by great muscular weakness (without atrophy) and progressive fatigability. It is due to a functional abnormality, lack of acetylcholine or excess of cholinesterase at the myoneural junction, in which nerve impulses fail to induce normal muscle contractions. Unknown Etiology. More common in females. Occurs most frequently between ages of 20 and 50.

Occupational Therapist

One who evaluates the self care, work, play and leisure time task performance skills of well and disabled clients of all ages; plans and implements programs, social and interpersonal activities designed to restore, develop and maintain the client's ability to accomplish satisfactorily those daily tasks required of his specific age and necessary to his particular role adjustment.

Occupational Therapist Assistant

One who works under the supervision of the occupational therapist in evaluating clients, planning and implementing programs designed to restore or develop a client's self-care, work, play or leisure time task performance skills. Although the assistant requires supervision in conducting a remedial program, he can function independently when conducting a maintenance program.

Occupational Therapy
The use of work-related skills to treat or train the physically or emotionally ill, to prevent disability, to evaluate behavior and to restore disabled persons to health, social or economic independence.

Osteogenesis, Osteogeny
Formation and development of bone taking place in connective tissue or in cartilage. Imperfecta is an inherited disorder of connective tissue characterized by defective bone matrix with calcification occurring normally on whatever matrix is present. Clinical findings are: multiple fractures with minimal trauma, blue sclerae, early deafness, opalescent teeth, tendency to capillary bleeding, translucent skin, and joint instability. Although the disease is heterogeneous, two different classifications of osteogenesis imperfecta are still used for clinical distinction: osteogenesis imperfecta congenita with early fractures occurring even in utero; and osteogenesis imperfecta tarda with delayed onset of fracturing and much milder manifestations. Healing of bone fractures progresses normally. Later in life, the tendency to fracture decreases and often disappears. The vast majority of cases are inherited as an autosomal dominant trait although a small percentage of congenital cases are transmitted as an autosomal recessive. There is no known cure for osteogenesis imperfecta; therefore, treatment is still supportive and palliative.

Paraplegic
Paralysis of lower portion of the body and of both legs. A lesion involving the spinal cord which may be due to the following: maldevelopment, epidural abscess, hematomyelia, acute transverse myelitis, spinal neoplasms, multiple sclerosis, syringomyelia, or trauma. 1. Ataxic-Lateral and posterior sclerosis of the spinal cord characterized by slowly progressing ataxia and paresis. 2. Peripheral—Paraplegia due to pressure on, injury to, or disease of peripheral nerves. 3. Spastic—Paraplegia characterized by increased muscular tone and accentuated tendon reflexes. Seen in multiple sclerosis and other conditions involving the pyramidal tracts.

Physical Therapist
An individual who is legally responsible for planning, conducting and evaluating a physical therapy program for patients referred by physicians.

Physical Therapist Aide
An individual with on-the-job training and experience who performs routine tasks under direction of the physical therapist.

Physical Therapist Assistant
An individual who works within a physical therapy service carrying out a planned program under the direction of a physical therapist.

Physical Therapy
Rehabilitation concerned with restoration of function and prevention of disability following disease, injury or loss of body part. The therapeutic properties of exercise, heat, cold, electricity, ultraviolet rays and massage are used to improve circulation, strengthen muscles, encourage return of motion and train or retrain an individual to perform the activities of daily living.

Poliomyelitis
Inflammation of the gray matter of the spinal cord. The complications are paralysis, atrophy of muscles, and ultimate deformities. Aside from bronchopneumonia, which may develop in very severe cases, other complications are surprisingly few.

Psychiatrist
A physician who specializes in study, treatment, and prevention of mental disorders.

Psychiatry
The branch of medicine which deals with diagnosis, treatment, and prevention of mental illness.

Psychologist
One who is trained in methods of psychological analysis, therapy, and research.

Psychology
The science dealing with mental processes, both normal and abnormal, and their effects upon behavior. There are two main approaches to the study: introspective, looking inward or self-examination of one's own mental processes, and objective, i.e., studying the minds of others.

Quadraplegia
Paralysis of all four extremities and usually the trunk. Etiol: Injury to the spinal cord, usually at the level of the 5th or 6th cervical vertebra. The injury may be higher but death occurs when damage is above the level of the 3rd cervical vertebra.

Rehabilitation
The processes of treatment and education that lead the disabled individual to attainment of maximum function, a sense of well being and a personally satisfying level of independence. The person requiring rehabilitation may be disabled from a birth defect or from an illness. The combined efforts of the individual, family, friends, medical, nursing, allied health personnel, and community resources make rehabilitation possible.

Sex
1. The characteristics which differentiate males and females in most plants and animals. 2. Motivation, both psychological and physiological, for behavior associated with procreation and erotic pleasure.

Sexuality
1. State of having sex; the collective characteristics which mark the differences between the male and the female. 2. Constitution and life of individual as related to sex; all the dispositions related to the love life whether associated with the sex organs or not.

Speech
1. Verbal expression of one's thought. 2. The act of uttering articulate words or sounds. 3. Words that are spoken. It is thought that certain crude sounds served as warnings or threats

in much the same way as did facial and bodily expressions. As sounds became highly differentiated, each became associated, and gradually identified with a certain idea. These word–symbols are a most valuable tool in ideation, and thinking is very largely dependent on this internal speech. Further identifications have made possible visual symbols (written language); though primitive written language was entirely unrelated—a series of pictures and crude representations. External speech requires the coordination of larynx, mouth, lips, chest, and abdominal muscles. These have no special innervation for speech but the upper neurons respond to complex motor pattern fields which convert the idea into suitable motor stimuli.

Speech Pathologist
An individual who is prepared by education and training to plan, direct and conduct programs to improve communicative skills of children and adults with language and speech impairments arising from physiologic disturbances, defective articulation or dialect. This individual can evaluate programs and perform research related to speech and language problems.

Speech Therapy
The study, diagnosis and treatment of defects and disorders of the voice and of spoken and written communications.

Spina-Bifida
Any spinelike protuberance. Congenital defect in walls of the spinal canal caused by lack of union between the laminae of the vertebrae. Lumbar portion is section chiefly affected.

APPENDIX III

Doctors Doing Research Related to Sex and the Handicapped

Cole, Theodore M., MD.
Department of Physical Medicine
   and Rehabilitation
University of Michigan
Ann Arbor, Michigan 48106

Davis, Sanders, M.D.
Institute of Rehabilitation
   Medicine
New York University Medical
   Center
New York, New York 10016

Glass, Dorothea, M.D.
Department of Physical Medicine
   and Rehabilitation
Temple University
Moss Rehabilitation Center
Philadelphia, Pennsylvania 19122

Halstead, Lauro, M.D.
Baylor University
Texas Institute for Rehabilitation
   and Research
Houston, Texas 77025

Hohmann, George, Ph.D.
V.A. Hospital
Tucson, Arizona 85713

Manley, Scott, Ph.D.
Craig Rehabilitation Hospital
Englewood (Denver), Colorado
   80201

Mayclin, Dan, Ph.D.
Santa Clara Valley Medical
   Center
San Jose, California 95103

Rosen, Joel, M.D.
Rehabilitation Institute of
   Chicago
Northwestern University
Chicago, Illinois 60601

APPENDIX IV

Federal and National Headquarters of Service Agencies

Department of Health,
  Education and Welfare
South Portal Building
200 Independence Avenue SW
Washington, D.C. 20201

Health Services Administration
Parklawn Building, Room 14–15
5600 Fishers Lane
Rockville, Maryland 20857

National Institutes of Health
9000 Rockville Pike
Bethesda, Maryland 20205

Offices of Education
400 Maryland Avenue SW
Washington, D.C. 20202

Office of Human Development
200 Independence Avenue SW
Washington, D.C. 20201

Rehabilitation Services
  Administration
330 C Street SW
Washington, D.C. 20201

Social Security Administration
6401 Security Boulevard
Baltimore, Maryland 21235

Closer Look:
  An Information Center
  for Parents of
  Handicapped Children
P.O. Box 1492
Washington, D.C. 20013

The National Association
  for Mental Health, Inc.
1800 North Kent Street
Arlington, Virginia 22209

The National Easter Seal Society
  for Crippled Children and
  Adults
2023 West Ogden Avenue
Chicago, Illinois 60612

United Cerebral Palsy
  Associations, Inc.
66 East 34th Street
New York, New York 10016

Service Agencies by State

ALABAMA
State Department of Education
501 Dexter Avenue
Montgomery, Alabama 36130

Division of Rehabilitation
and Crippled Children
2129 East South Boulevard
P.O. Box 11586
Montgomery, Alabama 36111

Mental Health Association
in Alabama
306 Whitman Street
Montgomery, Alabama 36104

Alabama Society for Crippled
Children and Adults, Inc.
2125 East South Boulevard
P.O. Box 6130
Montgomery, Alabama 36106

United Cerebral Palsy Association
of Alabama
2430 11th Avenue N.
Birmingham, Alabama 35234

ALASKA
Department of Health
and Social Services
Pouch H
Juneau, Alaska 99811

Department of Education
State Office Building
Pouch F
Juneau, Alaska 99811

Alaska Mental Health
Association
5401 Cardona Street, Suite 304
Anchorage, Alaska 99503

Easter Seal Society for Alaska
Crippled Children and Adults
1345 West 9th Avenue
Anchorage, Alaska 99501

ARIZONA
Department of Economic
Security
1717 West Jefferson Street P.O.
Box 6123
Phoenix, Arizona 85007

Family Health Services
Arizona's Children's Hospital
200 North Curry Road
Tempe, Arizona 85281

Mental Health Association
   of Arizona
341 West McDowell Road
Phoenix, Arizona 85003

Easter Seal Society for
   Crippled Children and Adults
   of Arizona, Inc.
706 North First Street
Phoenix, Arizona 85004

ARKANSAS
Department of Education
Arch Ford Building
State Capitol Mall
Little Rock, Arkansas 72201

Department of Human Services
Division of Mental Retardation/
   Developmental Disabilities
   Services
Waldon Building, Suite 400
7th and Main Streets
Little Rock, Arkansas 72201

Division of Rehabilitation
   Services
1401 Brookwood Drive
P.O. Box 3781
Little Rock, Arkansas 72203

Mental Health Association
   in Arkansas
420 Leake Building
121 East 4th Street
Little Rock, Arkansas 72201

Easter Seal Society for
   Crippled Children and Adults
   of Arkansas, Inc.
2801 Lee Avenue
Little Rock, Arkansas 72205

United Cerebral Palsy
   of Arkansas, Inc.
1607 South Main Street
Little Rock, Arkansas 72206

CALIFORNIA
Department of Developmental
   Services
744 P Street
Sacramento, California 95814

Department of Rehabilitation
830K Street Mall
Sacramento, California 95814

Department of Social Services
744 P Street
Sacramento, California 95814

California Mental Health
   Association
1211 H Street, Suite F
Sacramento, California 95814

Easter Seal Society for
   Crippled Children and Adults
   of California
742 Market Street, Suite 202
San Francisco, California 94102

United Cerebral Palsy
   of California
120 N. El Camino Real
San Mateo, California 94401

COLORADO
Department of Education
State Office Building, Room 523
Denver, Colorado 80203

Department of Social Services
1575 Sherman Street
Denver, Colorado 80203

Division for Developmental
Disabilities
4150 S. Lowell Boulevard
Denver, Colorado 80236

Mental Health Association
of Colorado
22 Clayton Street
Denver, Colorado 80206

Easter Seal Society for
Crippled Children and Adults
of Colorado, Inc.
609 W. Littleton Boulevard
Littleton, Colorado 80120

CONNECTICUT
Department of Education
165 Capitol Avenue
Hartford, Connecticut 06115

Department of Health Services
79 Elm Street
Hartford, Connecticut 06115

Department of Social Services
110 Bartholomew Avenue
Hartford, Connecticut 06115

Mental Health Association
of Connecticut
56 Arbor Street
Hartford, Connecticut 06106

Easter Seal Society of
Connecticut, Inc.
P.O. Box 1013
Jones Street
Amston, Connecticut 06231

United Cerebral Palsy Association
of Connecticut, Inc.
P.O. Box 3874
Amity Station
New Haven, Connecticut 06525

DELAWARE
Division of Public Health
Jesse Cooper Building
Dover, Delaware 19901

Division of Social Services
Box 309
Wilmington, Delaware 19899

Division of Vocational
Rehabilitation
Department of Labor
State Office Building
820 North French Street
Wilmington, Delaware 19801

Mental Health Association
in Delaware
1813 North Franklin Street
Wilmington, Delaware 19802

Easter Seal Society for
Crippled Children and Adults
of Del-Mar, Inc.
2705 Baynard Boulevard
Wilmington, Delaware 19802

United Cerebral Palsy
of Delaware, Inc.
P.O. Box 44
Wilmington, Delaware 19899

DISTRICT OF COLUMBIA
Department of Human Resources
415 12th Street, NW, Room 407
Washington, D.C. 20001

Division of Special Education
Webster Administration Building
10th & H Streets, NW
Washington, D.C. 20001

Mental Health Administration
1875 Connecticut Avenue, NW,
  Room 824
Washington, D.C. 20009

District of Columbia
  Mental Health Association
2101 16th Street, NW
Washington, D.C. 20009

District of Columbia Society
  for Crippled Children, Inc.
2800 13th Street, NW
Washington, D.C. 20009

United Cerebral Palsy
  of Washington, D.C.
1501 Columbia Road, NW
Washington, D.C. 20009

FLORIDA
Department of Health and
  Rehabilitative Services
1323 Winewood Boulevard
Tallahassee, Florida 32301

Vocational Rehabilitation
  Program Office
1309 Winewood Boulevard
Tallahassee, Florida 32301

Social and Economic
  Services Office
1311 Winewood Boulevard
Tallahassee, Florida 32301

Mental Health Association
  of Florida
132 East Colonial Drive, #207
Orlando, Florida 32801

Easter Seal Society for
  Crippled Children and Adults
  of Florida, Inc.
State Road 46, Route 1
Box 350
Sorrento, Florida 32776

United Cerebral Palsy
  of Florida, Inc.
309 Office Plaza, Suite 101
Tallahassee, Florida 32301

GEORGIA
Department of Education
State Office Building
Atlanta, Georgia 30334

Department of Human
  Resources
State Office Building
47 Trinity Avenue SW
Atlanta, Georgia 30334

Developmental Disabilities
  Council
618 Ponce de Leon Avenue
Atlanta, Georgia 30308

Georgia Easter Seal
  Society for Crippled Children
  and Adults, Inc.
3254 Northside Parkway NW
Atlanta, Georgia 30327

HAWAII
Department of Health
P.O. Box 3378
Honolulu, Hawaii 96801

Department of Social Services
P.O. Box 339
Honolulu, Hawaii 96809

Department of Education
P.O. Box 2360
Honolulu, Hawaii 96804

Mental Health Association
of Hawaii
200 North Vineyard, #101
Honolulu, Hawaii 96817

Easter Seal Society for
Crippled Children and Adults
of Hawaii
710 Green Street
Honolulu, Hawaii 96813

United Cerebral Palsy of Hawaii
245 North Kukui Street, Suite
208
Honolulu, Hawaii 96817

IDAHO
Department of Education
Len B. Jordan Building
Boise, Idaho 83720

State Board for
Vocational Education
650 West State Street
Boise, Idaho 83720

Department of Health
and Welfare
State House
Boise, Idaho 83720

Mental Health Association
of Idaho
3105½ State Street
Boise, Idaho 83703

Easter Seal Society for
Crippled Children and Adults
of Idaho, Inc.
1090 Federal Way
Boise, Idaho 83705

United Cerebral Palsy
of Idaho, Inc.
100 North Latah
Boise, Idaho 83704

ILLINOIS
Department of Rehabilitation
Services
623 East Adams Street
Springfield, Illinois 62705

Division of Services
for Crippled Children
University of Illinois
540 Iles Park Place
Springfield, Illinois 62718

Illinois Office of Education
100 North 1st Street
Springfield, Illinois 62777

Illinois Mental Health
Association
1418 South F Street
Springfield, Illinois 62703

Easter Seal Society of Illinois
for Crippled Children
and Adults, Inc.
P.O. Box 1767
Springfield, Illinois 62705

United Cerebral Palsy of Illinois
309 South 3rd Street
Springfield, Illinois 62701

INDIANA
Department of Public Instruction
State House, Room 229
Indianapolis, Indiana 46204

Department of Public Welfare
State Office Building, Room 701
Indianapolis, Indiana 46204

Rehabilitation Services Board
Illinois Building
17 West Market Street
Indianapolis, Indiana 46204

Mental Health Association
in Indiana
1433 North Meridan Street
Indianapolis, Indiana 46202

Indiana Easter Seal Society
for Crippled Children
and Adults, Inc.
3816 East 96th Street
Indianapolis, Indiana 46240

United Cerebral Palsy of Indiana
445 North Pennsylvania Street
Indianapolis, Indiana 46204

IOWA
State Services for Crippled
Children
The University of Iowa
Iowa City, Iowa 52242

Department of Public Instruction
Grimes Office Building
Des Moines, Iowa 50319

Developmental Disabilities
Program
523 East 12th Street
Des Moines, Iowa 50319

Mental Health Association of
Iowa
315 East Fifth Street, Suite 5
Des Moines, Iowa 50309

Easter Seal Society for
Crippled Children and Adults
of Iowa, Inc.
P.O. Box 4002
Highland Park Station
Des Moines, Iowa 50333

United Cerebral Palsy of Iowa
423 South West 8th Street
Des Moines, Iowa 50309

KANSAS
Cripples Children's Program
202 Century Plaza Building
111 West Douglas
Wichita, Kansas 67202

Department of Social and
Rehabilitation Services
State Office Building
Topeka, Kansas 66612

Department of Education
120 East 10th
Topeka, Kansas 66612

Department of Human Resources
401 Topeka Avenue
Topeka, Kansas 66603

Mental Health Association
of Kansas
1205 Harrison
Topeka, Kansas 66612

Easter Seal Society for
Crippled Children and Adults
of Kansas, Inc.
3701 Plaza Drive
White Lakes Plaza West
Topeka, Kansas 66609

United Cerebral Palsy
of Kansas, Inc.
P.O. Box 8217
Wichita, Kansas 67208

KENTUCKY
Department of Education
Capital Plaza Tower
Frankfort, Kentucky 40601

Department for Human
Resources
275 East Main Street
Frankfort, Kentucky 40621

Bureau for Social Services
275 East Main Street, 6W
Frankfort, Kentucky 40621

Kentucky Mental Health
Association
310 West Liberty Street, #106
Louisville, Kentucky 40202

Kentucky Easter Seal Society
for Crippled Children
and Adults, Inc.
P.O. Box 1170
Louisville, Kentucky 40201

United Cerebral Palsy Association
of Kentucky
P.O. Box 5481
Lexington, Kentucky 40505

LOUISIANA
Office of Health Services and
Environmental Quality
P.O. Box 60630
New Orleans, Louisiana 70160

Office of Human Development
P.O. Box 44371
Baton Rouge, Louisiana 70804

Department of Education
State Education Building
P.O. Box 44064
Baton Rouge, Louisiana 70804

Mental Health Association
in Louisiana
1528 Jackson Avenue
New Orleans, Louisiana 70130

Easter Seal Society for Crippled
Children and Adults
of Louisiana, Inc.
P.O. Box 8425
Metairie, Louisiana 70011

United Cerebral Palsy
of Louisiana
1710 Franklin Street
Gretna, Louisiana 70053

MAINE
Department of Education
Education Building
Augusta, Maine 04333

Bureau of Rehabilitation
32 Winthrop Street
Augusta, Maine 04330

Pine Tree Society for
  Crippled Children and Adults,
  Inc.
84 Front Street
Bath, Maine 04530

MARYLAND
Department of Education
P.O. Box 8717
B.W.I. Airport
Baltimore, Maryland 21240

Department of Health
  and Mental Hygiene
201 West Preston Street
Baltimore, Maryland 21201

Maryland Mental Health
  Association, Inc.
325 East 25th Street
Baltimore, Maryland 21218

United Cerebral Palsy Association
  of Maryland
213 Duke of Gloucester Street
Annapolis, Maryland 21401

MASSACHUSETTS
Department of Education
31 Saint James Avenue
Boston, Massachusetts 02116

Division of Family
  Health Services
39 Boylston Street
Boston, Massachusetts 02116

Department of Social Services
150 Causeway Street
Boston, Massachusetts 02114

Rehabilitation Commission
Statler Office Building
20 Providence Street
Boston, Massachusetts 02116

Massachusetts Mental
  Health Association
1 Walnut Street
Boston, Massachusetts 02108

Easter Seal Society for
  Crippled Children and Adults
  of Massachusetts, Inc.
37 Harvard Street
Worcester, Massachusetts 01608

MICHIGAN
Bureau of Rehabilitation
P.O. Box 30010
Lansing, Michigan 48909

Department of Education
P.O. Box 3008
Lansing, Michigan 48909

Department of Social Services
300 South Capitol Avenue
Lansing, Michigan 48926

Mental Health Association
  in Michigan
15920 West Twelve Mile Road
Southfield, Michigan 48076

Easter Seal Society for
Crippled Children and Adults
of Michigan, Inc.
10601 Puritan Avenue
Detroit, Michigan 48238

United Cerebral Palsy
of Michigan, Inc.
202 East Boulevard Drive
Flint, Michigan 48503

MINNESOTA
Department of Education
Capitol Square Building
550 Cedar Avenue
St. Paul, Minnesota 55101

Department of Health
717 Delaware Street, SE
Minneapolis 55440

Department of Public Welfare
Centennial Office Building
St. Paul, Minnesota 55155

Mental Health Association
of Minnesota
6715 Minnetonka Boulevard,
Room 209–210
St. Louis Park, Minnesota 55426

United Cerebral Palsy
of Minnesota, Inc.
1821 University Avenue, Suite
380 S.
St. Paul, Minnesota 55104

MISSISSIPPI
Board of Health
P.O. Box 1700
Jackson, Mississippi 39205

Department of Education
P.O. Box 771
Jackson, Mississippi 39205

Vocational Rehabilitation
Division
P.O. Box 1698
Jackson, Mississippi 39205

Mental Health Association
in Mississippi
Box 5041
Jackson, Mississippi 39216

Easter Seal Society for
Crippled Children and Adults
of Mississippi, Inc.
P.O. Box 4958
3226 N. State
Jackson, Mississippi 39216

United Cerebral Palsy
of Mississippi
P.O. Box 2264
Jackson, Mississippi 39205

MISSOURI
Division of Vocational
Rehabilitation
3523 N. Ten Mile Drive
Jefferson City, Missouri 65101

Department of Social Services
Broadway State Office Building
Jefferson City, Missouri 65101

Department of Mental Health
2002 Missouri Boulevard
P.O. Box 687
Jefferson City, Missouri 65102

Mental Health Association
in Missouri
411 Madison Street
Jefferson City, Missouri 65101

Easter Seal Society for
Crippled Children and Adults
of Missouri
8124 Delmar Boulevard
St. Louis, Missouri 63130

United Cerebral Palsy of Missouri
P.O. Box 611
Columbia, Missouri 65201

MONTANA
Department of Social and
Rehabilitation Services
P.O. Box 4210
Helena, Montana 59601

Mental Health Association
of Montana
201 S. Last Chance Gulch
Helena, Montana 59601

Easter Seal Society for
Crippled Children and Adults
of Montana
4400 Central Avenue
Great Falls, Montana 59401

United Cerebral Palsy
Association of Montana, Inc.
1601 2nd Avenue North
Casco Building, Room 432
Great Falls, Montana 59401

NEBRASKA
Department of Education
P.O. Box 94987
Lincoln, Nebraska 68509

Services for Crippled Children
P.O. Box 95026
Lincoln, Nebraska 68509

Easter Seal Society for
Crippled Children and Adults
of Nebraska, Inc.
P.O. Box 14204
Omaha, Nebraska 68114

United Cerebral Palsy of
Nebraska
1600 North 56th Street
Lincoln, Nebraska 68504

NEVADA
Department of Human Resources
Capitol Complex
505 East King Street
Carson City, Nevada 89701

Department of Education
Capitol Complex
400 West King Street
Carson City, Nevada 89701

Easter Seal Society for
Crippled Children and Adults
of Nevada, Inc.
2915 East Sunrise Street
Las Vegas, Nevada 89101

NEW HAMPSHIRE
Department of Health and
Welfare
Health and Welfare Building
Hazen Drive
Concord, New Hampshire 03301

Department of Education
State House Annex
Concord, New Hampshire 03301

Developmental Disabilities
Council
Health and Welfare Building
Hazen Drive
Concord, New Hampshire 03301

Easter Seal Society—Goodwill
Industries of New Hampshire,
Inc.
870 Hayward Street
Manchester, New Hampshire
03103

Granite State United
Cerebral Palsy Association
815 Elm Street, Room 54
Manchester, New Hampshire
03101

NEW JERSEY
Department of Human Services
P.O. Box 1237
Trenton, New Jersey 08625

Division of Medical Assistance
and Health Services
324 East State Street
P.O. Box 2486
Trenton, New Jersey 08625

Division of Youth
and Family Services
P.O. Box 510
Trenton, New Jersey 08625

Department of Labor
and Industry
John Fitch Plaza
Trenton, New Jersey 08625

New Jersey Mental Health
Association
60 South Fullerton Avenue
Montclair, New Jersey 07042

Easter Seal Society for
Crippled Children and Adults
of New Jersey, Inc.
166 Main Street
Lakewood, New Jersey 08701

United Cerebral Palsy
Association of New Jersey, Inc.
91 South Harrison Street
East Orange, New Jersey 07018

NEW MEXICO
Division of Vocational
Rehabilitation
P.O. Box 1830
Santa Fe, New Mexico 87503

Department of Health
and Environment
P.O. Box 948
Santa Fe, New Mexico 87503

Department of Human Services
P.O. Box 2348
Santa Fe, New Mexico 87503

Easter Seal Society for
Crippled Children and Adults
of New Mexico, Inc.
4805 Menaul, NE
Albuquerque, New Mexico 87110

United Cerebral Palsy
Association of New Mexico
205 San Pedro, NE
Albuquerque, New Mexico 87108

NEW YORK
Department of Health
Tower Building
Empire State Plaza
Albany, New York 12237

Office of Mental Health
44 Holland Avenue
Albany, New York 12229

Department of Education
Education Building
Albany, New York 12234

New York State Mental
Health Association
250 West 57th Street
New York, New York 10019

Association for Crippled Children
and Adults of New York State,
Inc.
855 Central Avenue
Albany, New York 12206

United Cerebral Palsy of
New York State
815 Second Avenue, 10th Floor
New York, New York 10017

NORTH CAROLINA
Department of Public Instruction
217 West Jones Street
Raleigh, North Carolina 27611

Department of Human Resources
325 North Salisbury Street
Raleigh, North Carolina 27611

Division of Health Services
P.O. Box 2091
Raleigh, North Carolina 27602

Division of Vocational
Rehabilitation Services
620 North West Street
P.O. Box 26053
Raleigh, North Carolina 27611

North Carolina Mental
Health Association
3701 National Drive, #222
Raleigh, North Carolina 27612

Easter Seal Society for
Crippled Children and Adults
of North Carolina, Inc.
832 Wake Forrest Road
Raleigh, North Carolina 27604

United Cerebral Palsy
of North Carolina, Inc.
417 North Boylan Avenue
Raleigh, North Carolina 27603

NORTH DAKOTA
Social Service Board
State Capitol
Bismarck, North Dakota 58505

Crippled Children's Services
Russel Building, RR 1
Bismarck, North Dakota 58505

Department of Public
Instruction
State Department of Public
Instruction
Bismarck, North Dakota 58501

Vocational Rehabilitation
Services
1424 West Century Avenue,
Suite 202
P.O. Box 1037
Bismarck, North Dakota 58505

North Dakota Mental Health
Association
Kirkwood Office Tower
Bismarck, North Dakota 58501

Easter Seal Society for
Crippled Children and Adults
of North Dakota, Inc.
Box 490
Bismarck, North Dakota 58501

United Cerebral Palsy
of North Dakota
319½ 5th Street North, Suite B
Fargo, North Dakota 58102

OHIO
Department of Health
246 North High Street
P.O. Box 118
Columbus, Ohio 43215

Division of Special Education
933 High Street
Worthington, Ohio 43085

Rehabilitation Services
Commission
4656 Heaton Road
Columbus, Ohio 43229

Mental Health Association
of Ohio
50 West Broad Street, #713
Columbus, Ohio 43215

Ohio Easter Seal Society for
Crippled Children and Adults,
Inc.
2204 South Hamilton Road
P.O. Box 27129
Columbus, Ohio 43227

United Cerebral Palsy
of Ohio, Inc.
1552 Loneaton Drive
Columbus, Ohio 43220

OKLAHOMA
Department of Education
2500 North Lincoln Boulevard
Oklahoma City, Oklahoma 73105

Department of Institutions,
Social and Rehabilitative
Services
P.O. Box 25352
Oklahoma City, Oklahoma 73125

Southwest Medical
5514 South Western, Suite #9
Oklahoma City, Oklahoma 73109

Oklahoma Society for
Crippled Children, Inc.
2100 Northwest 63rd Street
Oklahoma City, Oklahoma 73116

United Cerebral Palsy
Association of Oklahoma
5400-B North Independence
Street
Oklahoma City, Oklahoma 73112

OREGON
Department of Human Resources
Public Service Building
Salem, Oregon 97310

Mental Health Division
2575 Bittern Street, NE
Salem, Oregon 97310

Vocational Rehabilitation Division
2045 Silverton Road, NE
Salem, Oregon 97310

Crippled Children's Division
University of Oregon Health
  Sciences Center
P.O. Box 574
Portland, Oregon 97207

Department of Education
700 Pringle Parkway, SE
Salem, Oregon 97310

Mental Health Association
  of Oregon
718 West Burnside Street, #301
Portland, Oregon 97209

Easter Seal Society for
  Crippled Children and Adults
  of Oregon
4343 SW Corbett Avenue
Portland, Oregon 97201

United Cerebral Palsy
  Association of Oregon
7117 SE Harold Street
Portland, Oregon 97206

PENNSYLVANIA
Department of Education
Harrisburg, Pennsylvania 17126

Department of Public Welfare
P.O. Box 2675
Harrisburg, Pennsylvania 17120

Department of Labor and
  Industry
Labor and Industry Building
7th and Forster Streets
Harrisburg, Pennsylvania 17120

Mental Health Association
  in Pennsylvania
1207 Chestnut Street
Philadelphia, Pennsylvania 19107

Easter Seal Society for
  Crippled Children and Adults
  of Pennsylvania
P.O. Box 497
RFD 1
Fulling Mill Road
Middletown, Pennsylvania 17057

United Cerebral Palsy
  of Pennsylvania
1718 North Second Street
Harrisburg, Pennsylvania 17102

RHODE ISLAND
Department for Children
  and Their Families
610 Mount Pleasant Avenue
Providence, Rhode Island 02908

Vocational Rehabilitation
40 Fountain Street
Providence, Rhode Island 02903

Office of Commissioner
  of Education
100 Promenade Street
Providence, Rhode Island 02908

Mental Health Association
  of Rhode Island
55 Hope Street
Providence, Rhode Island 02906

Easter Seal Society for
  Crippled Children and Adults
  of Rhode Island, Inc.

667 Waterman Avenue
East Providence, Rhode Island
  02914

United Cerebral Palsy
  of Rhode Island
300 Knight Street
Warwick, Rhode Island 02886

SOUTH CAROLINA
Department of Social Services
P.O. Box 1520
Columbia, South Carolina 29202

Department of Health and
  Environmental Control
J. Marion Sims & R. J. Aycock
  Building
2600 Bull Street
Columbia, South Carolina 29201

Department of Vocational
  Rehabilitation
Landmark Center, Room 301
3600 Forest Drive
P.O. Box 4945
Columbia, South Carolina 29240

Department of Education
1429 Senate Street
Rutledge Building
Columbia, South Carolina 29201

South Carolina Mental
  Health Association
1823 Gadsden Street
Columbia, South Carolina 29201

Easter Seal Society for
  Crippled Children and Adults
  of South Carolina, Inc.
3020 Farrow Road
Columbia, South Carolina 29203

SOUTH DAKOTA
Department of Health
Joe Foss Building
Pierre, South Dakota 57501

Department of Social Services
Richard F. Kneip Building
Illinois Street
Pierre, South Dakota 57501

Department of Vocational
  Rehabilitation
Richard F. Kneip Building
Pierre, South Dakota 57501

South Dakota Mental
  Health Association
101½ South Pierre Street
Box 355
Pierre, South Dakota 57501

Easter Seal Society for
  Crippled Children and Adults
  of South Dakota, Inc.
106 West Capitol
P.O. Box 297
Pierre, South Dakota 57501

United Cerebral Palsy
  of South Dakota
RR 5
Box 244
Huron, South Dakota 57350

TENNESSEE
Department of Education
Cordell Hull Building
Nashville, Tennessee 37219

Division of Vocational
  Rehabilitation
1808 West End Building, Room
  1400
Nashville, Tennessee 37203

Crippled Children's
Service Program
Tennessee Department of Public
Health
State Office Building
Ben Allen Road
Nashville, Tennessee 37216

Tennessee Mental
Health Association
250 Venture Circle
Nashville, Tennessee 37228

Easter Seal Society for
Crippled Children and Adults
of Tennessee, Inc.
2001 Woodmont Boulevard
P.O. Box 15832
Nashville, Tennessee 37215

TEXAS
Department of Mental Health
and Mental Retardation
P.O. Box 12668
Austin, Texas 78711

Department of Human Resources
John H. Reagan Building
Austin, Texas 78701

Rehabilitation Commission
118 East Riverside Drive
Austin, Texas 78704

Mental Health Association
in Texas
103 Lantern Lane
Austin, Texas 78731

Easter Seal Society for
Crippled Children and Adults
of Tennessee, Inc.
4429 North Central Expressway
Dallas, Texas 75205

United Cerebral Palsy
Association of Texas
San Jacinto Building, Suite 201
221–223 East 9th
Austin, Texas 78701

UTAH
Department of Health
150 West North Temple Street
P.O. Box 2500
Salt Lake City, Utah 84110

Board of Education
1050 University Club Building
136 East South Temple
Salt Lake City, Utah 84111

Utah Mental Health Association
1370 South West Temple
Salt Lake City, Utah 84115

Easter Seal Society for
Crippled Children and Adults
of Utah, Inc.
4868 S. State Street
Murray, Utah 84107

VERMONT
Department of Education
Montpelier, Vermont 05602

Department of Social and
Rehabilitation Services
State Office Building
Montpelier, Vermont 05602

The Vermont Achievement
Center
P.O. Box 488
Rutland, Vermont 05701

VIRGINIA
Department of Health
James Madison Building
109 Governor Street
Richmond, Virginia 23219

Department of Rehabilitative
  Services
4901 Fitzhugh Avenue
Richmond, Virginia 23230

Department of Education
1322–28 East Grace Street
Richmond, Virginia 23216

Mental Health Association
  of Virginia
1806 Chantilly Street, Suite 203
Richmond, Virginia 23230

Easter Seal Society for
  Crippled Children and Adults
  of Virginia, Inc.
4841 Williamson Road
P.O. Box 5496
Roanoke, Virginia 24012

United Cerebral Palsy
  of Virginia, Inc.
The Jefferson Hotel
Box 1397
Richmond, Virginia 23211

WASHINGTON
Department of Social
  and Health Services
Mail Stop 440
Olympia, Washington 98504

Department of Education
State Superintendent's Office
Old Capitol Building
Olympia, Washington 98501

Easter Seal Society for
  Crippled Children and Adults
  of Washington, Inc.
521 Second Avenue West
Seattle, Washington 98119

Mental Health Association
  in Washington
P.O. Box 4008
2450 Star Lake Road
Federal Way, Washington 98003

WEST VIRGINIA
Department of Education
Capitol Complex
Building B–358
Charleston, West Virginia 25305

Board of Vocational Education
Division of Vocational
  Rehabilitation
State Capitol Building
Charleston, West Virginia 25305

Department of Health
1800 Washington Street East
Charleston, West Virginia 25305

West Virginia Mental Health
  Association
702½ Lee Street East
Charleston, West Virginia 25301

Easter Seal Society for
  Crippled Children and Adults
  of West Virginia, Inc.
1210 Virginia Street East
Charleston, West Virginia 25301

United Cerebral Palsy of
  West Virginia, Inc.
P.O. Box 1561
Charleston, West Virginia 25326

WISCONSIN
Department of Health
   and Social Services
State Office Building, Room 663
1 West Wilson Street
Madison, Wisconsin 53702

Division of Health
State Office Building, Room 280
1 West Wilson Street
Madison, Wisconsin 53702

Division of Vocational
   Rehabilitation
131 West Wilson Street, 7th
   Floor
Madison, Wisconsin 53702

Division for Handicapped
   Children
Department of Public Instruction
126 Langdon Street
Madison, Wisconsin 53702

Wisconsin Mental Health
   Association
119 E. Mifflin Street
Box 1486
Madison, Wisconsin 53701

Easter Seal Society for
   Crippled Children and Adults
   of Wisconsin, Inc.
2702 Monroe Street
Madison, Wisconsin 53711

United Cerebral Palsy
   of Wisconsin
315 West Gorham
Madison, Wisconsin 53703

WYOMING
Department of Health and
   Social Services
Hathaway Building
Cheyenne, Wyoming 82002

Department of Education
Hathaway Building
Cheyenne, Wyoming 82002

APPENDIX VI

Other Agencies for the Handicapped

American Diabetes
   Association, Inc.
600 5th Avenue
New York, New York 10020

American Heart Association
7320 Greenville Avenue
Dallas, Texas 75231

American Orthoptic and
   Prosthetic Association
1440 N Street, NW
Washington, D.C. 20005

American Physical Therapy
   Association
1156 15th Street, NW
Washington, D.C. 20005

American Spinal Injury
   Association
Northwestern Memorial Hospital,
   Room 580
250 East Superior
Chicago, Illinois 60611

Arthritis Foundation
3400 Peachtree Road, NE
Atlanta, Georgia 30026

Epilepsy Foundation
   of America
1828 L Street, NW, Suite 406
Washington, D.C. 20036

Foundation for Children
   with Learning Disabilities
99 Park Avenue, Second Floor
New York, New York 10016

National Association of the
   Physically Handicapped
76 Elm Street
London, Ohio 43140

The National Foundation—
   March of Dimes
1275 Mamaroneck Avenue
White Plains, New York 10605

National Hemophilia Foundation
25 West 39th Street
New York, New York 10018

National Multiple Sclerosis
   Society
205 East 42nd Street
New York, New York 10017

National Paraplegia Foundation
333 North Michigan Avenue
Chicago, Illinois 60601

New York Institute for
Child Development
205 Lexington Avenue
New York, New York 10016

Spina Bifida Association
of America
343 South Dearborn Street,
Room 319
Chicago, Illinois 60604

American Association for
Rehabilitation Therapy, Inc.
P.O. Box 93
North Little Rock, Arkansas
72116

Congress of Organizations
of the Physically Handicapped
6106 North 30th Street
Arlington, Virginia 22207

National Association of
Rehabilitation Facilities
5530 Wisconsin Avenue, Suite
955
Washington, D.C. 20015

The President's Committee on
Employment of the
Handicapped
Washington, D.C. 20210

American Association of
Special Educators
107–20 125th Street
Richmond Hill, New York 11419

American Coalition of Citizens
with Disabilities
1200 15th Street, NW, Suite 201
Washington, D.C. 20005

American Mental Health
Foundation, Inc.
2 East 86th Street
New York, New York 10028

American Vocational
Association, Inc.
2020 North 14th Street
Arlington, Virginia 22201

Committee for the Handicapped
People-To-People Program
1522 K Street, NW, Room 1130
Washington, D.C. 20005

The Council for Exceptional
Children
1920 Association Drive
Reston, Virginia 22091

Federation of the Handicapped
211 West 14th Street
New York, New York 10011

Mainstream
1200 15th Street, NW
Washington, D.C. 20005

National Association of State
Directors of Special Education
1201 16th Street, NW, Suite
610E
Washington, D.C. 20036

National Center on
Educational Media and
Materials for the Handicapped
Ohio State University
Columbus, Ohio 43210

Parents Campaign for
Handicapped Children and
Youths
Box 1492
Washington, D.C. 20013